THE D.Y GUIDE TO PUBLIC RELATIONS

2nd Edition

MOI ALI

A DIRECTORY OF SOCIAL CHANGE PUBLICATION

Published by
The Directory of Social Change
24 Stephenson Way
London NW1 2DP
Tel: 0171 209 5151, fax: 0171 209 5049
e-mail: info@d-s-c.demon.co.uk
from whom further copies and a full publications
list are available.

The Directory of Social Change
is a registered charity No. 800517.

First published 1995. Second edition 1999

ISBN 1 900360 53 5

British Library Cataloguing-in-Publication Data
A catalogue record for this book is available from
the British Library

Designed and typeset by Kate Bass and Midlands
Book Typesetting Company
Printed by Page Bros., Norwich

ABOUT THE AUTHOR

Moi Ali runs her own PR consultancy, The Pink Anglia Public Relations Company, which specialises in communications, marketing services and PR training for voluntary organisations and the public sector. She has over 15 years' experience in public relations, working not only for charities and voluntary organisations, but also for membership organisations, large companies, a government quango and two financial PR consultancies.

Moi is the author of a number of books on PR and marketing, including the DIY Guide to Marketing for Charities and Voluntary organisations, published by the Directory of Social Change.

Moi is a member of the Institute of Public Relations, the professional body which represents PR practitioners.

ACKNOWLEDGEMENTS

Thanks to Becky Glenister and Charles Collett at Charity Fair for their helpful comments and tips on exhibitions. Special thanks to Andrew Anderson for his invaluable comments on the manuscript.

Dedicated to Spike

CONTENTS

INTRODUCTION

There are some excellent PR books around, though most are either too theoretical, or written for commercial organisations. The case studies used in them, and the budgets they talk of, are not meaningful to the voluntary sector. This book is different because it is written specially for you by someone who specialises in charity PR.

It is tailor-made for groups who are new to public relations and who have limited budgets for PR activity, but it also contains much good advice and practical tips for bigger charities with less restricted PR budgets. It will help you to get the most from your PR spend and will show you how to develop your own PR programmes in order to be more effective at promoting your organisation and your services.

Designed to be as interactive and user-friendly as possible, the emphasis is on the practical: how to do it – and how not to do it! Containing a wealth of both fictitious examples and true stories, this book is based not on dry theory, but what you can expect in the real world, with plenty of tips and hints on how to do it better, and how to save money!

Although the examples given are based on the work of charities, the book's tips and advice are as relevant to the public sector and even small businesses as to the voluntary sector.

It is very much a working guide which has been designed so that it can be easily dipped into. Read it from cover to cover if you wish, or just look up chapters as you need to. It's your very own PR tool kit, and it's up to you how you use the tools it contains, and how you apply them to your own situation.

As well as tools, there are exercises which give you a chance to practise your PR skills in private, before you try them out on your own organisation.

By promoting your own work professionally, you are helping to create a positive image for the voluntary sector, which has in the past been too easily dismissed as being run by a bunch of 'do-gooders'. Shaking off that old image, and setting out to be taken seriously, is what this book is all about.

Good luck with your PR.

CHAPTER ONE

AN INTRODUCTION TO PUBLIC RELATIONS

In this chapter you can find out about public relations in general, what it is, and what it can do for you. There's a look at image development, and you can discover how to put together a PR strategy for your organisation.

WHAT IS PUBLIC RELATIONS?

What comes to mind when you think about a PR consultant? The stereotype is that they are loud-mouthed *poseurs* with Southern accents, continually on their mobile phones, swigging G&Ts or champagne between calls, and speeding from one superficial and gimmicky event to another in their GTi cabriolets, the roof down in all weathers. Some are like this, but most are not. The comedy TV series *Absolutely Fabulous* did little for the image of the PR consultant, but don't let that put you off.

So that's the consultant, but what about PR? How often have you heard people (and particularly politicians) dismiss something as "a PR exercise"? PR is often seen as the poor relation of marketing and advertising, probably because so few people really know what it is. The trouble is that so many people *think* they know what PR is. And if public relations is misunderstood by the public, it is certainly misunderstood by many voluntary organisations.

Most big companies make great use of PR techniques to boost their image and increase profits, but some of their PR activities have helped give PR a bad name and have made caring organisations wary. This is a pity, because PR can benefit an organisation, not by hyping its achievements, but by getting it to take a critical look at itself. By seeing your organisation as others see you, you can make yourself come across better, and you can ensure that you are providing the best possible service to your users.

Even many of those who do have some understanding of PR wrongly believe that it is just about media relations, but as you will see from the contents of this book, that is only a part of it. The official definition of PR, from the Institute of Public Relations, is:

"the planned and sustained effort to establish and maintain goodwill and mutual understanding between an organisation and its publics."

What does this mean for voluntary organisations and charities? PR for you is about projecting the image or personality of your organisation to

ORGANISATION: Save the Osprey

PUBLICS: conservation groups; bird watchers and ornithology clubs; pet shops; environmental groups such as Friends of the Earth and Greenpeace; bird and wildlife sanctuaries; schools; countryside groups; endangered species groups such as the Worldwide Fund for Nature; MPs and MEPs; Young Farmers; existing members and individual supporters; corporate sponsors; the wider public; the media; staff; volunteers; trustees.

your own 'publics' – users, supporters, funders, the local community, and to your other audiences, such as, perhaps, your local council, other voluntary organisations, and not forgetting your staff and volunteers too. As soon as you try to list your publics, you will find that you have many more than you realise, and that they are much more wide-ranging than you imagined, as the fictitious example in the box alongside shows:

So PR is about getting your message across to your publics, but it's a two-way process. You must communicate with your audiences, but you need to make it easy for them to talk to you too. One-way communication is just hype, which makes people think in terms of "PR stunts" and the like. Real PR involves dialogue – you need to listen to others, to see things from their perspective, and to take on board their criticisms and complaints, particularly if they are users of your service.

Why bother with PR?

As a voluntary organisation you rightly regard your role as that of service provider, or campaigner, or fundraiser, or pressure group, or whatever, but in order to get the funding to do what you do, you need to achieve a profile – with funders and supporters such as local authorities, central government, other organisations, and the public. In an increasingly competitive market, with more organisations but no more money, it's those with the profile that often secure the funding. It might be unfair, but it's the reality.

Some charities are understandably wary of PR. As I have said, they wrongly believe that PR is about hyping achievement. They understand it to be about a glossy image; they think it's about hiding flaws and shortcomings in their organisation. Many large, and some would say unethical, companies use PR in this way; other big companies use PR properly, to improve what they are doing and to provide a better service to the public.

There will always be people who will grumble about charities spending money on PR, people who regard it as an expensive luxury, or as completely unnecessary or inappropriate. Many donors and members of the public believe that every penny of a charity's income should go direct to the cause: they are reluctant to fund administration and would baulk at the notion of cash going into PR. But if you embark on a well thought-out, enlightened and carefully structured PR campaign which produces positive benefits, you will give such people no excuses for complaining; you may even get them to pause for thought and to rethink their attitude to PR.

Looking through their eyes

Good PR can result in an improved service for your customers and users: by focusing on their needs, and seeing things from their point of view, you can do what you do better. That's what lies at the heart of PR. It's about listening to others and developing a two-way process based on mutual trust and understanding.

You need to see your organisation as it is seen by others, and to involve users and supporters in improving it. A good starting point is to talk to your audiences and to find out what they think about you. Ask users of your service for ideas on how things can be improved. Find out from members how you could be more interactive with them. Talk to supporters about what they would like to see. And ask staff too. It's amazing how many good ideas they will have, but without positive encouragement, they may not be forthcoming. Use suggestions and comment boxes to elicit ideas, or write to staff and users asking them what they think. By looking critically at yourself through others' eyes, you can introduce improvements in many areas of your work. You can become better at communicating and at listening.

Sometimes you need to be proactive in seeking others' views; sitting back and waiting will seldom produce results. One way of finding out what people think is to produce a questionnaire, which can be done easily in-house. Decide what information you would like to get and design questions that will elicit it.

> **TRUE STORY**
>
> One organisation frequently held brainstorming sessions for managers in a bid to elicit ideas on how to run the company better. Sadly it never thought to involve other staff, and as a result it missed out on many valuable ideas. Finally, it introduced a suggestions scheme for all staff, and the first idea to come in was from a secretary who had devised a more efficient system for mail shots. Her idea, which resulted in savings of hundreds of pounds a year for the company, is one she had thought about for years, but she felt it was not her place to make such suggestions. The introduction of the suggestion scheme signalled to her that her ideas would at last be welcomed and valued.

You can mail your self-completion questionnaires, though don't expect a good return; professional market researchers are pleased with a response rate of 30% for postal questionnaires (you may get as few as 10% back), so you could be wasting valuable resources if you opt for this. Questionnaire return rates are increased if a stamped addressed envelope is enclosed, though this does add considerably to the cost of the exercise. (To avoid expenditure on wasted stamps, talk to Royal Mail about a freepost address, so that you will pay the cost of postage only on those returned.) A cost-effective alternative is to leave questionnaires in reception, where you have a captive audience with nothing better to do! Remember to have a box available for them to post the questionnaire in, plenty of pens, and space for their own additional comments.

There's an example of a simple questionnaire on the next page.

DIDDINGSTON DROP-IN CENTRE: HELP US TO BE BETTER!

We would like to improve our service and we need YOUR help. As someone who uses the Drop-in Centre, you are well placed to tell us how we are doing and what more we can do to make it even better, so please spare a few minutes to complete this questionnaire.

1. What do you think about the range of activities on offer at the drop-in centre?
   (Tick any of the descriptions that fit)
   ☐ Too many to choose from   ☐ Not enough choice   ☐ Just right
   In general, the activities are: ☐ Boring   ☐ Inappropriate for me   ☐ OK   ☐ Good
   Any other comments about the activities?
   _____

2. Are there any activities you would like us to run? (Please list them)
   _____

3. How often do you use the centre?
   ☐ Every day   ☐ Every week   ☐ At least once a month   ☐ Other (please state)

4. Would you use the centre more often if the activities offered were more relevant to you?
   ☐ Yes   ☐ No   ☐ Not applicable to me

5. What do you think of the centre café? (Tick any responses which apply)
   ☐ Too expensive for me   ☐ Good value   ☐ Affordable   ☐ Good food   ☐ Food OK
   ☐ Food poor ☐ Nice atmosphere ☐ Uncomfortable ☐ Untidy tables ☐ Pleasant ☐ Clean
   Any other comments on the café?
   _____

6. What do you think of the café staff? (Tick anything applicable)
   ☐ Friendly   ☐ Helpful   ☐ Professional   ☐ Unhelpful   ☐ Unfriendly   ☐ Good   ☐ OK
   Any other comments on the café staff?

7. Do you have any ideas for making the café better? What are they?
   _____

8. Would you use the centre more often if the café were better?   ☐ Yes   ☐ No

9. What do you like most about the Drop-in Centre?
   _____

10. What do you least like about the Centre?
    _____

11. Do you have any comments or ideas for making the Centre better?
    _____

Thank you for completing the questionnaire. Your views will help us to shape a better service. If we may get back to you to discuss your ideas, please complete your name, address and telephone number. You are, though, welcome to remain anonymous if you prefer.

**Please place this in the box at reception or return by post, by Feb. 19th, to:
The Drop-in Centre, High Street, Diddingston**

QUESTIONNAIRE CHECKLIST

■ Keep it as short as you can: people are put off by anything too long.

■ Make sure your address is on the questionnaire, so people know where to return it.

■ Give respondents the opportunity of returning the questionnaire anonymously if you want really truthful feedback!

■ Ensure that your questions are unambiguous and easy to understand.

■ Arrange questions in a logical order.

■ Ensure your questions are not biased or slanted. If respondents feel you have already made up your mind about the sort of answers you want, they may not bother to complete the questionnaire.

■ Ensure that the layout of your questionnaire is clear and easy; if it looks a mess, it will put people off filling it in.

■ Make it as easy as possible to complete, by giving boxes to tick or multiple choice options to circle.

■ Limit the number of open-ended questions, for they are difficult to process and off-putting to respondents.

■ Leave space for additional comments.

■ Have a deadline for the return of completed questionnaires.

> **TIP**
>
> *When designing your questionnaire, try to opt for questions and a format that will make it easier for you to collate the results in numerical or percentage terms. You want to be able to present your findings in a meaningful way. For example – over half of the respondents said that they would use the centre more often if the courses on offer were more relevant. Nearly one third of these people suggested assertiveness as a course they would like to see run.*

> **TIP**
>
> *Before setting your questionnaire loose on the public, do a trial run first. This will give you a chance to check for ambiguity and clarity of questions and will enable you to correct any errors. Try it out on friends and colleagues, or on a sample of potential respondents.*

IMAGE MATTERS

So-called 'spin doctors' have given 'image' a bad image! Many people believe that image is about window-dressing, a cosmetic presentation that lacks substance. Words like 'manipulation', 'whitewash' and 'distortion' spring to mind. Yet taking control of your image should not mean concealing flaws and hyping achievement. A close examination of your image can result in an improved service for your clients/service-users, bigger donations for your charity, more success in attracting funding ... the benefits go on and on.

If your image is stuffy and old-fashioned, but your service is aimed at young people, you are on to a loser. Your service might be just the thing that young people need, but if they don't see it that way, they will not approach you. You will be wasting your time. If you are seen as a white middle-class organisation, even if you are an equal opportunities employer, you are unlikely to get black people applying to you for jobs. So image is an issue for you.

Developing and then portraying the right image cannot be done overnight; it takes time and is a process rather than an event. You cannot suddenly become trendy, child-friendly, multi-racial or appealing to older users, but you must start somewhere and some time, and the best starting point is where you are now.

ASSESSING YOUR IMAGE

Set up a PR task group. Ensure that it represents a cross-section of your organisation, comprising, as appropriate:

- staff (not just the managers!)
- volunteers
- trustees or committee members
- service-users/clients
- customers
- donors

Each will bring a different perspective with them. Get the group to brainstorm the image you currently have. Next, ask the group to list every aspect of your organisation that is a manifestation of your image. If you were assessing a person's image, you might look at the way they dress, the music or books they like, their home and car, the way they speak and so on. What will you need to examine to assess your organisation's image? Once you have produced your list, assess each item and what it says about you. Your own list might include:

1. Your Leaflets and other Publicity Material

What do your publications say about you? Are they over-long and full of jargon, or clear, concise and in plain English? Carry out a review of your publications. Gather all of the printed material you produce – leaflets, annual report, letterheads, compliments slips, brochures – and see what image they promote. Look closely at:

design – What image does the design convey about your organisation? Is it good? Is it appropriate for the target audience?

copy – Is the language used appropriate for the audience? Is the writing style and tone right? How does it make your organisation sound? Friendly? Officious?

photographs and the illustrations – What images are used? What messages are conveyed by your choice of photographs or illustrations? Is a good cross section of the community represented? Is there an over-emphasis on pictures of staff?

What would you think about your organisation if you received these things and had no other knowledge on which to base your view?

2. Your Premises

A good image starts in your reception area. Is yours comfortable, or draughty and littered with dog-eared magazines and posters for events which have long since taken place? Can you do anything to improve access – is it easy for people with pushchairs or in wheelchairs? Pop into reception now and try to look at it as a stranger would see it. What impression does it convey of your organisation? Is that the image you want?

Like your home, your premises – where they are and how they look – say a lot about your organisation. You probably cannot afford plush offices and would regard them as inappropriate anyway. You can, however, create a pleasant reception and office space on a limited budget, even if your premises are dreary and cramped. With a bit of imagination, a tin of bright paint, a stencil, a few framed prints and some pot plants, you can go a long way towards creating a better environment. Visitors and staff will appreciate it, and it will enhance your image.

Keeping offices clean and tidy is important too, creating a more professional and organised feel. You would be unimpressed if you visited an office that was untidy and disorganised, with files lying everywhere, messy desks, the smell of stale chips in the air, dirty coffee mugs on every surface and a motley collection of dead plants on the windowsill. Such offices do not inspire confidence; indeed they probably cause visitors to question the organisation's competence.

Equally, you should avoid appearing too opulent, though this is generally not a problem for most charities! A marble reception counter, deep-pile carpets and designer curtains would make you appear profligate, extravagant and wasteful. Donors would have cause to question how their money was being spent. It is not difficult to get the balance right, creating a comfortable, businesslike and efficient office that avoids being too swish. (Once you get your office looking right, make sure you hold meetings there so others can see it. Consider holding an open day, too.)

> **TIP**
>
> *When reviewing your printed material, take the opportunity to decide whether you really need all of these leaflets and publications. Also identify any gaps. Perhaps you could make do with a general leaflet: that brochure on your organisational strategy may be unnecessary.*

> **TIP**
>
> *If your office is difficult to find, or off the beaten track, produce a map showing where it is and how to get there. Mark on it useful information such as bus stops, train stations and car parks, as well as local landmarks to orientate people. This way your visitors will not arrive late, flustered and determined to hold the next meeting at their place!*

3. Your Job Advertisements

Is your application form for employment easy to complete? What image does it convey about you? I recently saw a printed application form which had a space on it labelled 'Honours'. It gave me the distinct impression that the organisation valued honours - such as the OBE etc. - on a par with experience. I found this distinctly off-putting and wondered whether they were out to attract a certain type of person.

4. Notices and Signs in your Premises

Sometimes notices and signs can let down an otherwise friendly and caring organisation. Officious and unfriendly signs will not enhance your image. Take a look at notices and check that they do not hector, lecture or order your visitors. Express yourself in a friendly and helpful style.

5. The Way you Welcome Visitors

Do visitors receive a warm welcome from a friendly and helpful receptionist or are they lucky if they get a grunt and a nod? The role of frontline staff, such as receptionists and telephonists, is so often overlooked, and yet they are fundamental to good PR. They are often the only contact people have with you, so the image they convey can be all-important. Your whole organisation may be judged on their performance.

TRUE STORY

I was interested in applying for a job with a large charity a few years ago. The application form asked so many irrelevant personal questions about marital status, medical history and dependants that I decided this was not the sort of organisation I would like to work for. The job sounded great, but the application form let the organisation down. How many good candidates failed to apply because of it?

---

6. The Way your Phone is Answered

Get a friend to telephone your organisation and to assess what image comes across over the phone. Is your telephonist/ receptionist helpful, knowledgeable and professional? Are callers put through to the right extension first time? Are extension phones answered promptly and courteously? Test and see.

7. Correspondence

The written word is every bit as important as the spoken word. Check a cross-section of correspondence to see what image comes over. Are your letters over-formal or unfriendly in style? Is correspondence answered promptly and fully? If it is not, your image will be harmed and you will get a reputation for being inefficient and unhelpful.

8. Your Answer Machine

Listen to the message on your office answer machine. What does this say about you? Could you improve it? If so, do so!

9. Your Patron

Your choice of patron or president will also have an impact on your image. In their eagerness to attract an honorary leader with a title, many charities overlook the effect their choice will have on their image. A traditional, conservative charity might benefit from selecting Lord So-and-So or Lady Hobnob, for it does add credibility, but for a charity aiming for a more upbeat, zippy image, this would be a poor choice! It is always a help to have a well known figurehead, but you do not have to limit yourself to the aristocracy – explore the world of theatre, TV and film, books, music and art. Though remember that deciding on a patron is quite different to persuading them to accept the title! You might regard it as the chance of a lifetime, but you are not doing them any favours, so don't expect them to jump at the prospect.

10. Your Trustees

Who you have as trustees and committee members is also an issue if you care about public perceptions of your organisation. The old days of committees comprising white, middle class professionals and do-gooders is over. Committees should bring together people with relevant experience and skills who are representative of your users and of wider society, avoiding tokenism at all costs. So get your committee right if you don't want to alienate potential supporters.

Look at every aspect of your work that has an impact on how you are perceived. Of course, what you come up with will be no more than your own perception of how you are seen. The only way to get a true picture is to ask others outside your charity, whether clients/users, supporters or other organisations. Doing this is time-consuming and usually best left to someone independent: people may be less inclined to give you their honest opinion if you approach them direct. You can get around this by sending out a questionnaire asking about your image, to be returned anonymously. (See above for information on questionnaires.)

> **TRUE STORY**
>
> The image gap landed the Body Shop in trouble in 1994. They had spent years promoting their 'green' image and there was a high awareness among the public that their products were environmentally friendly and cruelty-free. People regarded the Body Shop as an ethical company who they felt they could trust. When, however, a damning article appeared in the American press undermining many of the company's ethical claims, immense bad press followed throughout Britain and the States, and share prices plummeted.
>
> Many other cosmetic companies were guilty of far worse things than the Body Shop, but they have not promoted themselves as being 'green', nor spent vast sums of money in developing an ethical image. In their case there was no image gap. But the Body Shop was hoist by its own petard. It was only skilful damage limitation by the Body Shop's PR staff that saved the day.

For some organisations, a good test of how well-known you are and what sort of an image you have is to stand 500 metres from your office and to ask passers-by for directions to your premises. If you find that most people have never heard of you, or they say disparaging things about your organisation, you will be facing an uphill PR and promotions job, but at least your research will have told you something about your organisation, even if it is a rather unpalatable truth.

IMPROVING YOUR IMAGE

Once you have some idea of how you are regarded, think about the image you would like to have and compare it with the image you actually have. PR techniques can help you to bring the two into line.

When considering your desired image, make sure that you aim for something that is both realistic and achievable. There is no point in deciding that you are going to have the highest profile in your sector, that you want to be regarded as the biggest or the best, if this is simply not achievable. Write down your desired image. This is a good way of focusing your mind and clarifying your thoughts, and it's a useful check that you share the same understanding.

BLOW YOUR OWN TRUMPET

Companies are all too ready to sing their own praises, yet charities are surprisingly modest when it comes to publicising their achievements. Don't be shy – get your trumpet out and tell the world how good you are:

- issue a news release if you are commended or win an award
- frame award certificates and hang them where they can be seen
- leave a file of 'thank you' letters in reception for visitors to read
- keep a book of favourable press coverage in reception
- if you produce publications, enlarge and frame the reviews they receive

Go back and look at the areas of your work that you assessed. Which bits are letting you down? Where is there room for improvement? Draw up a list. For each item, write down what action is required to improve your image. For example, suppose you run a service for parents, yet you don't exactly have a child-friendly image. You might need to buy some toys and comics for your reception, organise crèches when you hold meetings, create a comfortable area for breast-feeding, and have a potty or two to hand.

Deciding what action is required is the first step. Next you must ensure that your image-improving ideas are implemented. The best way to guarantee action is to assign each task to a named individual and charge them with getting the job completed. Set a deadline and, if relevant, a budget too. Hold regular meetings to check on progress. On the next page you can see an example of how you might set out the findings of your image audit and record what action is required.

In all that you do, compare the image you would like to have with the one that you are actually projecting. The two should coincide, but if they do not, do something about it.

Beware the image gap

If the good image you promote for your organisation is not matched by the reality, you have an image gap and you are asking for trouble. Your hype will raise expectations among your publics, and when, inevitably, you fail to meet those expectations, you will leave everyone feeling disappointed, let down and cheated. That's why it is vital that the image and the reality coincide.

TEN INSTANT WAYS TO IMPROVE YOUR IMAGE

1. Re-record the message on your answering machine to make it more friendly and informative. If you don't have an answer machine, consider getting one.

2. Tidy your reception area and offices and keep them that way.

3. Greet visitors warmly, even if you are not pleased to see them! Ensure all staff do likewise.

4. Smile when you answer the telephone – it will make all the difference.

5. Place a full range of your leaflets and publicity in reception for visitors to take away. Also leave a copy of publications you sell, though mark them 'DO NOT REMOVE'!

ITEM	IMAGE	DESIRED IMAGE	ACTION REQUIRED	BY WHOM	BUDGET	BY WHEN
Tenants' handbook	Makes us sound very authoritarian. Design is very old fashioned	More friendly and modern.	Need to rewrite copy in a more friendly style. Need to get handbook redesigned to make it look fresher	Jackie to rewrite copy. Commission professional designer	£1,500 to include design and print	July 1st Get copy to designers by mid July for delivery in August
Reception	Dreary and unwelcoming	Welcoming and bright, but not too plush or expensive-looking	Repaint in sunny lemon colour. Put up framed drawings by tenants' children.	Maintenance Manager to arrange painting. Mary to organise paintings	£500	ASAP
Media image	Non-existent	Want a higher profile with positive coverage	Talk to PR consultants locally	Director to approach 3 consultants	Get soundings from consultants as to likely cost	June 30th
Image with tenants	They think that we are very uncaring and only interested in our own careers and in getting their rent money	To be regarded as a friendly, fair and a caring landlord	Hold open day so tenants can meet us. Undertake consultation with tenants to find out what they want from us (and act on the findings)	John Arif	£100 for publicity and refreshments. Only cost for consultation is staff time, but there may be costs involved in implementing findings	August 20th Start straight away

6.   If you have a backlog of mail, issue holding letters now. In future, respond to all mail promptly, or send out holding letters so your correspondents know they are not forgotten.

7.   Avoid using jargon when you speak and write.

8.   Keep a supply of leaflets in your bag and car, so there is always one to hand when you meet someone who is unfamiliar with your work.

9.   Display your office/opening hours clearly in your window, and any forthcoming dates when you will be closed, such as public holidays.

10. Talk to colleagues and find out what they are doing that is of interest, then issue a news release to promote it. (If you don't know what a news release is, read Chapter 3.)

STRATEGIC PR

Image development is one aspect of strategic public relations. 'Strategic' is one of those buzzwords that is overused, often wrongly applied and little understood. This is unfortunate, because the concept of strategic PR is fundamental to successful PR activity.

So many organisations say "Let's do some PR," or "We could do with a bit of good PR," without understanding that PR is not something that can be done *a la* Tommy Cooper – just like that! "Doing a bit of PR" is not an option; PR must be part of the organisational philosophy. It must, as the official definition of PR has it, involve planned and sustained effort.

Real PR does not just happen all by itself. Objectives need to be set, so that you are clear about what you hope to achieve from your PR and to enable you to evaluate its success. You must define your 'publics' or audiences, so that you can target your messages. Messages need to be written down, as a check that everyone in the organisation is in agreement about what image you are promoting and what you are saying to whom. Put all of this together in one document and you have the framework for a PR strategy. A very simple PR strategy is included on page 21, where we reproduce the strategy devised to market this book. (Your own strategy will be much longer and more complex, for it will cover all of your organisation's work, not just one aspect.)

Your strategy needs to include:

Where you are now

Start with a summary of where you are now, what PR activity you currently carry out and what sort of an image you think you have. This is your benchmark.

THE PR STRATEGY FOR THIS BOOK

AIMS
- to ensure maximum targeted media coverage of the book in order to alert potential readers to its existence
- to persuade people to buy the book

AUDIENCES
- individual charities and voluntary organisations
- organisations representing charities, such as NCVO, SCVO
- local authority and public sector PR departments
- health authorities and health boards
- community groups
- the wider PR profession
- small businesses

GENERAL MESSAGES
- the book is accessible, readable and comprehensive
- the book is worth buying

TAILORED MESSAGES: charities etc.
- the book is written specially for charities

TAILORED MESSAGES: health service
- the book contains many health service examples
- it was written by someone who has health service clients and connections

TAILORED MESSAGES: small businesses
- the book is ideal for small businesses and was written by someone who runs her own small business
- it is full of practical, cost-effective ideas that are relevant to small businesses

TAILORED MESSAGES: the PR profession
- the book is written by a member of the Institute of Public Relations
- the book is endorsed by the President of the IPR

TAILORED MESSAGES: public sector
- the book is highly relevant for the public sector, far more so than the many books written for large companies and commercial organisations

THE STRATEGY
- Demonstrate the book's authority by approaching relevant PR figures and seeking quotes/independent endorsements for the book jacket. Approach the President of the IPR, to show that it is a serious book. Approach the Head of PR at a leading charity, to demonstrate its relevance to charities
- Drum up advance interest in the book by getting as much coverage as possible in target publications
- Officially launch the book to ensure that everyone knows about it
- Use direct mail as a back-up to editorial coverage
- Exploit the Scottish connection to get coverage in Scottish publications – Sunday Times Scotland, local papers, ScotMedia, Scottish business press etc.

TIMETABLE

Sept '94	Approach Keith Henshall, President of the Institute of Public Relations for quote on book jacket Approach Sandra Horniman of NCH for quote on jacket
March '95	Approach Scottish Council for Voluntary Organisations to ask if they are interested in helping publicise the book when it is launched Issue tailored news releases announcing that the book has been commissioned
April '95	Directory of Social Change mails flyer to publicise the book
May '95	Launch the book by giving a talk to SCVO members on PR. Have copies available for sale Issue tailored releases announcing publication Seek reviews in target publications – PR Week, IPR Journal etc.

Where you want to get to

Next look at the image you would like to have by a given time. Ask "What image would we like to have by this time next year? What about in five years' time?" Plan short-term and long-term.

Objectives

Set yourself no more than half a dozen objectives, for example:

■ to improve our customer care for service users

■ to get more media coverage for our work in general, and particularly to attract positive and intelligent coverage about our projects for drug-users

■ to attract the interest of decision-makers

Your objectives should be realistic and your progress measurable.

Publics

List all of the audiences with whom you deal (your list will be longer than you think). Now group them into categories, e.g. decision-makers, other charities and voluntary organisations, customers/clients etc. and rank them in order of importance. Agree on no more than five that you need to target during the next 12 months and prioritise these.

Messages

You will probably find that you need to send different messages to different audiences. Alongside each audience that you have prioritised, list the essential messages that you must convey during the next year. For example:

Audience: Decision-makers

Messages: We are competent and professional, with a commitment to customer care and value for money. We are innovative and pioneering, with an eagerness to develop cost-effective solutions.

Audience: Clients

Messages: We are caring and supportive and always respect confidentiality. We have an 'open door' policy and will never turn anyone away. The service is free.

Timetable

Finally, once you are clear about what you hope to achieve you can plan your PR activity. Set down what you intend to do and when you plan to do it. For example:

July 1st	Launch new plain English promotional booklet.
August 20th	Open new service for drug-users. Hold media conference. Announce figures for drug rehabilitation scheme.
August 25th	Copy deadline for newsletter.
September 20th	Issue quarterly newsletter. Send copies to media with a news release highlighting newsworthy story.
October 1st	Start work on annual report. Assemble working group for planning annual conference.
December 4th	Publicise photographic competition.
December 16th	Assess PR successes and review strategy for next year.

Ensure that the events you are planning will help you meet your PR objectives, reach your target groups and promote your key messages. Set a date at the outset for reviewing your PR activity and evaluating its success.

Strategic PR takes considerable effort and planning and you may wonder how much time and money you should spend on it. This will vary from charity to charity, depending on your income, size, staff resources, and how high a priority you give PR. Getting your PR right will not lead to riches overnight, but it could ensure your long-term survival, and it should result in some kind of future payout – your raised profile may lead to increased donations, more successful campaigning, or more skilled volunteers; your better, responsive service should lead to more satisfied clients, to an increase in users and thus to more funding.

You should regard PR as one of the elements of your organisation's overall strategy. Time spent doing PR is an investment in its survival and development, and therefore an integral part of your everyday work. You make time and money available to do the payroll, the annual accounts, for staff training and so on, so set some aside for PR and prepare to reap the fruits – perhaps not immediately, but certainly in the long run.

A FINAL WORD

If PR is not for you, read this....

If you're a cynic, you've probably not managed to reach this far into the book. For those who have, here are a few arguments to persuade you that PR really is a must, not an optional extra.

You can see when an organisation cares about PR. It shows in their attitude to users and supporters. It can be seen in the way they deal with enquiries. You can tell by looking at their publications. The whole organisation cries out quality. It is well-organised, forward-thinking, focused and responsive. In short, it cares.

Such organisations generally do well because their professionalism and commitment comes across. They impress funders and supporters. They attract the best staff and volunteers – and keep them. They provide better services to clients, sell better products to supporters, produce better campaigning and information materials.

To be better in all these respects you need to take PR seriously. It's not a quick fix-it, it's a way of thinking. It's part of an organisation's ethos and approach, part of the whole philosophy. So if you care and you want your organisation to be better, read on.

CHAPTER TWO

INTERNAL PR

If you are to be successful at PR, you first need to get your own house in order. That means getting things right with your own staff – communicating well with them and encouraging them to take an interest in the organisation they work for and its PR objectives. Find out in this chapter how to keep staff in the know, how to make best use of 'honorary staff' such as volunteers, patrons and trustees, and how to make sure that staff do not let you down in your own PR.

Even if you plan to do no other PR, it is a good idea to get your internal public relations right, as it will help you to achieve a better relationship with your staff and will lead to many knock-on benefits.

Knowledgeable, informed staff who feel valued provide a better service and are more committed, much more motivated, less likely to be off sick and less likely to want to change jobs. They are more likely to be flexible in their approach and to put themselves out for you, so it makes sense to consider their needs. Enlightened organisations who regard their staff as people and not as machines recognise that staff have a right to be treated well and to know what is going on where they work.

The British car industry during the 1970s was notorious for its constant strikes and industrial relations problems. By contrast, the Japanese car manufacturers who set up here did very much better in this respect, and much of their success was put down to the fact that they kept staff informed, involved them in decision-making, and made them feel part of the company. Other foreign companies based in Britain, such as Ford, now pay great attention to staff and their information needs, employing a large communications team to keep everyone abreast of events and developments. You will not have at your disposal the resources of a large company, but that's no excuse for being a poor communicator.

The main area of communication breakdown in any organisation is between managers and staff. Too many managers assume that because they know something, other staff will know it too – which is generally not the case, even in quite small organisations. The organisational hierarchy means that many staff are denied quite basic and necessary information, whether intentionally or not. They have to rely on the grapevine, which, while it can be extremely effective, is also often a way of spreading false rumours and unhelpful speculation. Many a strike that should never have happened took place because people relied on the grapevine for their information, being starved of it by their seniors.

There are numerous organisations which have a caring image as far as the public is concerned, yet they are, unintentionally, poor employers, due in part to their poor communication systems, or even complete lack of them. Setting up a system should be easy if you are a small charity, but for bigger organisations, formal procedures need to be put in place to inform staff of news and developments. You can choose from:

Team Briefings – these are really suitable only for the larger charities. You write a brief, and line managers go through it with their staff. The advantage is that all staff receive the same message at the same time, so it is particularly useful for organisations spread across many sites or those with regional offices.

Staff Meetings – it's an old idea but a good one. Some charities ask staff to suggest topics to go on the agenda for the next meeting, giving staff a chance to air issues that are important to them.

Newsletters/news-sheets – these can be glossies or cheapo in-house efforts, they can appear at a frequency of your choosing, and can be chatty or formal. All it takes is a word processor and a photocopier!

Noticeboards – the humble noticeboard is so often overlooked as a communications tool. Get using yours now!

Staff Training Sessions – in-house sessions are a great way of bringing the team together and examining an issue or problem.

Question Time – this is a chance for staff to find out what they want to know. Make up a panel of managers/team leaders to field the questions and introduce an element of fun by getting the Chair to wear a Robin Day-style bow tie.

Roadshows – if you have lots of offices, staff not based at head office might feel neglected or isolated. Get off your butt and go and see them.

Listening Circles – this is where managers listen to staff and all of their concerns. It's a chance for staff to have a good moan in a non-threatening environment.

These are all useful ways of ensuring that staff know what is happening and understand why. As with other aspects of PR, internal communications is also two-way. It's all very well to talk to staff, but you need to listen to them too.

TRUE STORY

A national charity for disabled people ran a printing subsidiary to raise money. It won a contract from a company to print pornographic material, which it accepted in spite of staff objections. Staff tried to sort the matter out internally with management, but finally, in frustration, they went to the media. Headline coverage resulted in very damaging publicity for the charity and a tarnished image. In the end they were forced into reneging on they contract. If only they had listened to their staff!

INTERNAL COMMUNICATIONS QUESTIONNAIRES

If you are a large organisation with lots of staff, or many offices, it can be difficult to get communications right, or even to know where you are going wrong. The best way of uncovering communication blockages and stoppages is to carry out a staff communications questionnaire. An example of some of the questions you may want to consider can be found on the sample communications questionnaire overleaf.

Having found out what is happening in your organisation, and where communication is breaking down, publish the findings for staff and – most important of all – take steps to correct and improve your communications. Having highlighted the problem areas, it should be relatively easy to put procedures in place for addressing these. It is best to involve staff in devising ways of tackling communications problems, perhaps by setting up a communications review group which comprises representatives from all of your offices as well as different grades of staff, volunteers and perhaps a union rep.

Feedback to staff is crucial if you want their support in improving the way you operate internally. In feeding back the information to staff, try to set it out the main findings in a meaningful way. The sample feedback sheet on page 28 shows how you could tackle it.

> **TRUE STORY**
>
> A friend of mine was volunteering for a local charity. The staff treated her like a dogsbody, getting her to make the coffee, do all the photocopying and faxing, and generally treating her like an unpaid servant. They talked to each other as if she was not there and never involved her in anything interesting. Needless to say she left after just a few weeks. It was their loss. She is a very talented graphic artist and would have loved to have lent her skills to the charity, but no one spoke to her for long enough to find this out.

If staff are neglected when it comes to communications, volunteers get an even worse deal. You may not pay them, but they still work for you. You are relying on their goodwill, and you are more likely to secure that if you make them feel valued and informed team members. Invite them to staff meetings, to social events and to briefing sessions. Issue them with job descriptions, lay on induction sessions for new volunteers, and let them attend training courses. And if you have lots of volunteers, consider doing a newsletter specially for them – you can even get one of your volunteers to take responsibility for its production.

Internal communications is an area much overlooked, even by many charities with a good external profile. Surprisingly, it is also neglected by many big companies, perhaps because it is seen as being at the less glamorous end of PR. More enlightened companies, however, have been quick to cotton on to the benefits of good internal communications – fewer industrial relations problems, increased productivity, decreased absenteeism, better time-keeping – and there is now a lucrative internal communications industry with specialist consultants who collect fat fees for their expertise. There is no need for you to employ one of these

CHARITY FIRST COMMUNICATIONS QUESTIONNAIRE

Charity First is committed to good communication, and as a first step in improving communications across the board, is focusing on internal communications. Who better to ask for views than you, the staff? Tell us where we are going wrong and pass on your ideas for doing it better. You can do this by filling in and returning this questionnaire. We will publish the results in August and you will be sent a personal copy of the findings.

Many thanks for your help.

Margot Maddison
Director

1. In which part of Charity First do you work?
   ❏ Head Office   ❏ Manchester office   ❏ Edinburgh office   ❏ Warehouse

2. Is your job grade...   ❏ Grade 1–6   ❏ Grade 7–12

3. In addition to your immediate work team, with which part of Charity First do you identify most strongly?
   ❏ Your department   ❏ Your office/region   ❏ The organisation as a whole
   ❏ Other (please specify) _____

4. Please indicate whether you agree or disagree with the following statements. Tick only one box per statement.

	AGREE +/+	+	+/-	–	DISAGREE -/-
I feel isolated from other parts of Charity First	❏	❏	❏	❏	❏
My manager gives me all the information I need	❏	❏	❏	❏	❏
Communication within my work team is good	❏	❏	❏	❏	❏
I have to rely on the grapevine for the information I need	❏	❏	❏	❏	❏
I think my manager is interested in my views	❏	❏	❏	❏	❏
Management only tell us what they want us to know	❏	❏	❏	❏	❏
Communication works well between HQ and other offices	❏	❏	❏	❏	❏

5. How useful do you find each of the following as sources of information?

	VERY USEFUL	QUITE USEFUL	NOT USEFUL	DON'T KNOW
Team briefing	❏	❏	❏	❏
Staff newsletter	❏	❏	❏	❏
My manager	❏	❏	❏	❏
Noticeboards	❏	❏	❏	❏
Annual report	❏	❏	❏	❏
Memos	❏	❏	❏	❏
Noticeboards	❏	❏	❏	❏
Press cuttings	❏	❏	❏	❏
Other (Please specify)				
_____	❏	❏	❏	❏

6. In general, how satisfied are you with internal communications at Charity First?

SATISFIED +/+	+	+/-	–	NOT SATISFIED -/-
❏	❏	❏	❏	❏

7. If in general you are not satisfied with internal communications at Charity First, please indicate the main causes of this. You may tick more than one box.
   ❏ Not enough information   ❏ Too much information   ❏ Information received too late
   ❏ Inaccurate information   ❏ Not enough contact with my manager
   ❏ Not enough contact with other offices   ❏ Information which is not relevant to me

8. Do you have any suggestions for improving internal communications at Charity First? (please specify.)
   _____

9. Which of the following Charity First publications do you receive?
   ❏ Annual report   ❏ Staff newsletter   ❏ Leaflets

Thank you for completing this questionnaire. Please return your completed questionnaire in the envelope provided by Friday, July 17th.

CHARITY FIRST STAFF COMMUNICATIONS QUESTIONNAIRE
SUMMARY OF FEEDBACK

Thank you for taking the time to fill in the recently circulated communications questionnaire. The response was fantastic, with 95% of forms being returned by the deadline. Here is the promised feedback of the main findings.

■ We asked who, in addition to your workteam, do you most strongly identify with. Clearly we are failing to build a strong corporate feel, for only 5% of staff said that they most strongly identify with Charity First. Most of you identify most strongly with the office where you are based.

■ Those working at Head Office do not feel at all isolated from Charity First but staff in the regional offices do, to a large extent. The most isolated staff of all are those working in the warehouse.

■ Most of you feel that your manager gives you the information you need, though staff at Head Office are less happy in this respect. Managerial staff are generally better informed by their managers than are clerical staff.

■ While most of you feel that communication in your own work team is good, over 70% of staff are still having to rely on the grapevine.

■ Most of you (80%) believe that your manager is interested in your views, yet the same percentage think that managers only tell you what they want you to know.

■ Staff at Head Office think that communication between Head Office and the other offices is good, though 77% of staff in the regions strongly disagree.

■ The staff newsletter is the most useful source of information, followed closely by team briefing. The annual report is generally considered a poor information source.

■ Most of you are reasonably satisfied with internal communication at Charity Fair. Of the 10% who are not, managers cite the main cause of dissatisfaction as being information overload, while clerical grades say it is due to lack of information. Ideas suggested for improving communication range from management roadshows to the regional offices, to the use of electronic mail. All ideas put forward will be evaluated and there will be a round-up published in the next issue of the staff newsletter.

**Anyone wanting a copy of the full findings should contact
Michael McGurk at Head Office.**

consultants, even if you can afford to do so. Good internal communications is to a large extent about common sense.

STAFF AND YOUR IMAGE

Your staff are probably your most valuable asset. Improving communication with them is crucial to your public image, for your staff are your ambassadors. You are judged on their performance, so the impression they give will shape the image you have. Getting staff to recognise and accept their ambassadorial role is an important first step to improving your public image and to building their commitment. You cannot do this until you have developed within yourself and your charity an awareness of PR and its value.

As ambassadors, it is important that you and your staff look the part, for appearances do count, particularly outside the voluntary sector – among those you are trying to influence, attract funding from etc. In the private sector and among potential funders you will often find a preconceived idea about people who work in the voluntary sector. You will confirm their prejudices if you arrive for a meeting dressed like a train-spotter or wearing a little number you picked up for 10p at a jumble sale. Don't go overboard with power-dressing or designer outfits, but do dress appropriately for important meetings, public and TV appearances and so forth, if you want to be taken seriously and to make the right impact.

While staff can sometimes let an organisation down, damaging its reputation, it has to be said that organisations often let staff down. Any damage to reputation caused this way can only be described as self-inflicted. Many organisations, charities included, can behave well with their existing personnel, only to treat prospective staff very shabbily. An Industrial Society survey revealed that many organisations failed to write to applicants who were not shortlisted, treated interviewees discourteously, and were unnecessarily slow in telling applicants the outcome of their interviews. The author was quoted as follows: "Organisations will spend thousands of pounds on public relations, and yet many of them fail to understand that people who seek jobs with them will tell their family and friends if they have been poorly treated".

It is easy for those charities with poor administrative support and no budget for acknowledging job applications to be guilty of this. Make sure that you are not. It costs nothing to state in the job advert that an SAE should be enclosed, nor to be properly organised for interviews, and to be welcoming and professional. You should aim to leave those not offered a job with a feeling of disappointment, and correspondingly eager to apply to work for you in the future, not one of relief at a narrow escape.

When we think of staff, we generally have in mind those on the payroll. Volunteers often slip our minds, and our patrons, presidents, committee members and trustees are frequently completely forgotten, even though charities and voluntary organisations would find it impossible to get by without them. These people, who give up their time to support charity, open doors for organisations and provide the chance to tap into new networks. Treat them well.

Because they are on the periphery of your charity, you will have to take steps to keep them informed and involved; if you don't, they might feel undervalued and decide that they can think of better ways to spend their time. The more you put into your relationship with trustees, the more you will get out. Just like staff, valued trustees will work harder, they will be more committed, and will miss fewer committee meetings. So how can you achieve this? Here are a few ideas:

- invite them to your staff Christmas party and other social events

- send them a copy of your newsletter and other new publications

- ask them to your staff away day

- consider an open day or induction training for new committee members

- plan visits for them so that they can see your work in action

- issue new members with a briefing sheet outlining their role and responsibilities

- lay on special briefing events for them, though not too many, for they will have other commitments

The success of your organisation's PR lies in the commitment of your staff and voluntary staff (including trustees). Without everyone's support, you will be straining to create and maintain a good service and an image to match. Treat them well, keep them informed and involved and you will get the very best out of them. If you don't, you will damage their faith and they will damage your reputation.

TRUE STORY

A few years ago I applied for a job with a local public relations consultancy. I went to a lot of trouble preparing my application but received nothing in return, not even an acknowledgement. I phoned to check that they had received it, for I feared it might have been lost in the post. They said they would check and ring me back, but they didn't bother. Later that year I needed to engage a PR agency for a project I was working on: guess who was not on my list of possibles? If you treat potential employees this way, they won't support your charity in the future. Nor will anyone they tell.

CHAPTER THREE

MEDIA RELATIONS

In this chapter you can learn how best to deal with the media, from getting stories into newspapers to being interviewed on radio and television. There's a guide to who's who on a newspaper, tips on how to make your news releases more likely to be used, and information on how to monitor and evaluate coverage. You can even find out how to cope with the media in a crisis.

No Great Mystery

When people think of PR, media relations is often the first thing that comes to mind. It's by no means all that PR is about, but it is nevertheless an important part. Many people working in PR like to make out that there is a great mystery in dealing with the media. There isn't. Once you know the basics, you can quickly and easily develop a good working relationship with your local media, and the more often you achieve a success, the more confident you will feel about going to the media the next time.

By media we mean radio, television and newspapers (including trade publications). Since most charities most of the time will be dealing with local newspapers, that's the emphasis in this chapter.

HOW NEWSPAPERS WORK

When you read a story in the newspaper, or hear something on the radio or television, you may wonder how the media got hold of the story. A great deal of news is generated by news releases, which are issued by companies and increasingly by charities and pressure groups. A news release is simply a news story which has been set out in a particular style (see below). They used to be called press releases, but nowadays, with our broadcast media seeking out news from business and the community for an ever increasing number of programmes, press releases have become known as news releases. If you call yours a 'press release', you might alienate or irritate the broadcasters.

News Releases

Many local newspapers have a small staff, so they rely on news releases for much of their coverage. If you send in a good release, the chances are that it will get used verbatim. If you send relevant black and white photographs with your release (suitably captioned), these may also be used. Don't send photos to radio and television, though!

When a newspaper receives your release, they will do one of three things with it:

- They will use it, either word for word or having edited it a little

- They will telephone you for further information, and then write their own story

- They will bin it, because it is no good, irrelevant for their readership, arrived too late, or because they had too much news already

National newspapers receive hundreds of releases every day, so the competition is very stiff. Even local papers receive more than they can use, so you need to do everything you can to ensure that your release is the one that does not end up in the bin. One obvious way of increasing your chances of coverage in the local papers is to ensure that your release has a *local* angle. This is not a problem for small, community-based charities, but it can be for national ones. If you issue a national release (e.g. 'Every year over 3,000 children in Britain are abused by their baby-sitters....') to all the local papers in the country, it will probably not get used. If, however, you 'localise' your standard release, simply by amending the headline and opening paragraph, you will find that the extra coverage you receive makes it well worth the effort. The above example, localised, could read 'Every year around 200 children in the London area are.....' or 'Every year over 300 children in Scotland are...' It is time-consuming to do this, though thanks to word processors, easier than it would have been a few years ago, and it is extremely effective.

> **TIP**
>
> *When writing a release, include a quote in it from a named person. Newspapers like this, as it makes their readers believe that they actually interviewed you, when really they just used your release!*

If your release is not addressed to a named person, it will go to the news desk, where it will be looked at by the news editor. He or she will have neither the time nor the inclination to read all your release; they will just glance at the first paragraph, and if this looks interesting, they will read on. If it's a bore, or they don't understand it, it will land, within seconds, in the nearest waste paper basket.

Releases that look the part

There is a convention when it comes to setting out news releases. Many good releases end up in the bin because they fail to follow the convention and are therefore difficult for newspapers to use, so if you want to maximise your chances of getting into print, make sure that your release looks right.

- always **DOUBLE SPACE** your releases – so that they are easier to read and can be easily edited

- use **WIDE MARGINS** – to allow for editing and for the reporter to write notes and instructions for the sub-editor

- releases should always be **SINGLE SIDED** – never type on both sides of a sheet of paper, and talking of typing, make sure that your releases are typed. Hand-written releases are asking to be binned

- use your A4 **HEADED NOTEPAPER** for the top sheet, but plain white paper for continuation sheets

- keep releases short – preferably no more than **TWO PAGES**. Long releases are generally not read because newsrooms are too busy and news editors tend to suffer from information overload. If you need to include a lot of information, put it on a separate sheet as background briefing material

- don't use fancy **FORMATTING** – if you underline, put words in bold, italics, capitals and so on, you will make life difficult for the reporter, who will have to annotate your release with instructions to remove your formatting

- never **SPLIT** a sentence from one page to the next. Ideally, don't let a paragraph continue over the page

- **STAPLE PAGES TOGETHER** - it's easy for paper-clipped pages to get separated in a busy newsroom

Releases that live up to the part

Getting a release to look the part is only half the story. It also needs to be:

- **BRIEF:** it should be a short (preferably no more than a page long) and concise story, not an epic novel

- **SNAPPY:** use clear, positive language, and short words and sentences

- **RELEVANT:** stick to the essentials and don't explain everything – just enough to make the uninformed reader understand

- **JARGON-FREE:** jargon, clichés, hype, unexplained abbreviations, facts you are unsure of, should all be avoided

Other points to bear in mind with releases if you want them to be used:

- always **DATE** your release. If you don't, the news editor might bin it, believing it to be old news

- include at least one **CONTACT NAME** and **NUMBER**. Make sure the contact is available, easy to get hold of, and fully briefed. Also include a **HOME NUMBER**, as journalists keep strange hours and they can be extremely impatient. If they want to follow up your release, they will soon drop your story if no one answers the telephone after a couple of attempts

- don't try to write witty or clever **HEADLINES** for the national press – they will be re-written by the newspaper. Free newspapers don't mind headlines with puns, as long as they are good ones

- use **EMBARGOES** only if you really must – they can be an irritation to journalists. Embargoes can be useful, however, and if used properly, you will be doing reporters and yourself a service. They are valuable for complicated stories such as research reports and annual reports, where a reporter might wish to do some advance work on the story before publication of your report. They are also good if you are sending material to Forward Planning Departments in radio and television. Remember that there is always the danger that your embargo may be broken, although they are generally respected

If you follow these rules, your release is less likely to be binned. But why bother to send a release at all? What will you get out of it?

- Chances are that it will generate free, positive publicity. Even if it is not used, it will let local journalists know what you are up to and keep the name of your organisation in their memory.

- It can be better, initially, than a potentially irritating or ill-timed phone call or visit. It puts into the journalists' hands the information YOU want them to have, so it puts you in control.

- Local papers are often badly understaffed, so good releases are welcome time-savers for busy reporters.

- You can keep a copy, and if a journalist badly misquotes you or twists your story, you have got proof.

- They are easier to read and more logically ordered than a reporter's scribbled and often illegible shorthand notes. There's less chance that they will get your name or your organisation's name wrong from a release, or give your story the wrong emphasis.

THINK BIG . . . BUT NOT TOO BIG!

When you have a good story with media potential, should you aim nationally, regionally or locally? There is no ready-made formula: it all depends on how important an event or issue you are dealing with. Generally for the smaller charities and voluntary organisations, your contact will be with the local media, especially newspapers. This is much easier than dealing with the nationals and you are far more likely to achieve success. However, don't rule out the national media if you have something really newsworthy. Many small charities do make national news, though perhaps only once in their lifetime.

With a big story, or a very specialised one, it can be difficult to know where to send your releases. You probably know your local and trade media, but what about other publications? How do you find out what exists and where they are based? Fortunately, thanks to various specialist directories, this task is quite simple. There are directories listing trade, technical and consumer titles, local papers, TV and radio, national media, European media, and business publications. Entries include: the title of the publication (or name of radio/TV station), the names of the editor and any special correspondents; addresses, telephone and fax numbers; circulation details; frequency of publication. They can be organised alphabetically by title, under subject headings, or geographically. All of them are easy to use, many are available at reference libraries (you probably would not want to subscribe, as the cost is around £350 per year), and the best known are:

PR Planner UK: It lists national dailies, Sunday papers, local weeklies (by county), consumer magazines, trade and technical journals, radio and TV networks, stations and news agencies. Editors, correspondents, features and specialist writers are also listed. PR Planner also do a radio and TV programmes guide.

PIMS United Kingdom Media Directory: Similar to the above. They also do a United Kingdom Media Townslist, with newspapers, radio and TV organised alphabetically by town name under regional headings.

> **TIP**
>
> *The directories listed here issue updates quarterly, six-monthly or annually. Ask a local PR consultancy (or the in-house PR department of a large company) if they will donate you their old copies rather than throwing them out. It could save you a fortune.*

Editors: Editors is published in six volumes – national daily newspapers, Sunday papers, national news agencies and radio and television; business and professional publications; provincial newspapers; consumer and leisure magazines; town by region media guide; London correspondents of the foreign press.

Benn's: Similar to the above, Benn's comes in three volumes, UK, Europe and World (covering 221 countries). In addition to the usual information, Benn's also contains advertising rates, which can be useful if you want to measure column inches and work out how much that coverage would have cost you had you had to pay for it.

You can also get directories on disk now, although subscription is not cheap. The advantages, however, are that you can do searches of the entire UK media in seconds, you can easily print out personalised mailing lists, and you can produce labels to make distribution of news releases easier.

Write your release so that it can be chopped paragraph by paragraph from the bottom up, and still make sense. This is what often happens to releases and news stories if there is not enough space in the paper – they are brutally hacked at the end!

Read the papers you send your releases to, be familiar with the type of stories they run, and the sorts of photographs they use.

TABLOID VS. BROADSHEET

'Tabloid' and 'broadsheet' simply refer to the size of the paper, with tabloids being more square in size, like the *Sun*, and broadsheets being longer, more rectangular, such as the *Guardian*. However, people often refer to tabloids as 'the popular press', and regard their coverage as rather trivial and sensational. Conversely, the broadsheets are sometimes called 'the qualities' because of their more serious treatment of material.

When you are approaching the national press, remember that tabloids and broadsheets have very different readerships, styles and interests. Generally the tabloids will love anything to do with animals, children, personalities (especially TV and sport) and human interest. The qualities will be more interested in current trends, policies, politics and issues.

Be cautious about using tabloids, because they may well treat your story differently from the way it would be handled in the quality press, though don't overlook them either; they have a mass readership which you may want to reach. The treatment your story gets will be quite different, as you can see from the following fictitious example:

WOMEN SUPPORT EMBRYO RESEARCH

Women are in favour of the use of eggs culled from aborted foetuses, according to the findings of research published today. The Covington University study revealed that 90% of women sampled said that they believed childless couples should be given the opportunity to have children, even if that meant using eggs from aborted foetuses or from young women killed in accidents.

EGG-CITING FERTILITY IDEA HATCHED

By the next century we could see children being born to mothers who were themselves UNBORN! Or to mothers who were DEAD at the time of conception. Boffins in a high-tech egg lab are working on ways of taking eggs from aborted babies and dead women, and transplanting them. Women have given the treatment the thumbs up.

It's easy to tell which is which from the style.

FOLLOW UP

Depending on the release, it might be worth phoning a couple of days later to establish personal contact and to 'sell' your story. However, be careful not to be a nuisance when phoning the media – some journalists are easily irritated, and even the easy-going ones will get annoyed if you keep pestering them or you catch them as their copy deadline approaches. The best time to call a daily paper is between 10.30am and 11.30am, as this is the least busy period and reporters will have more time to talk and will be more receptive to news. Never call between 4pm and 7pm, when journalists are writing and checking their copy, or you will get short shrift. And another tip: don't bother to call Sunday newspaper journalists on a Monday – it's their day off.

Find out the deadline of your local papers. Bear these in mind when sending releases and planning events.

PRESS OFFICE ADMINISTRATION

Even if you don't employ a press officer or run a formal press office, there are certain systems you should have in place if you intend to use the media fairly often. First of all you must keep a copy of all your releases and a list of who you sent them to. This makes it easier for you to monitor your press coverage and to build up a picture of which papers (and indeed which reporters) are interested in your work. You can do your own press monitoring, or pay a cuttings agency to do it for you. (There is information on media monitoring companies further on in this chapter. Sample forms to help you with your monitoring and evaluation can be found there too.)

If you work in a larger organisation, you will probably want to keep a rein on the issuing of releases by your staff, perhaps by setting up systems for getting releases cleared by a relevant person before issue. You might find an adaptation of the sample form useful.

You should also log all contact with the media that is reactive. (There is a sample form that you can adapt on page 62.) This allows you to keep a track on who you have been contacted by, who responded, and what they said.

> **TIP**
>
> *Start a scrap book of press cuttings, with details of the date of the cutting and the publication in which it appeared, as it's nice to be able to look back over old clippings. It can give your organisation a sense of history, and your new staff an insight into your work over the years.*

GETTING IN THE PICTURE

If you want pictures taken at your event, include a 'NOTE TO PICTURE EDITOR' at the end of your release, saying when, where, and what photographs can be taken. (That's assuming that you are sending out a release in advance of the event happening.) Only do this if you have something photogenic on offer. Children, animals, funny outfits, props and giant things all make good pictures. Men in grey suits do not! You can phone the picture desk to see if they are sending a photographer.

If the paper is not sending anyone, you might decide to employ your own photographer to take some black and white prints for you to send to your local paper, but don't spend your money on this unless you have a good photo-story. Use a freelance photographer who works for your local paper, as they will have the right contacts and they are generally no more expensive than other photographers. Picture editors hate what they call "grip 'n' grins". These are photos of smiling people grasping a certificate/giant cheque/award. A picture editor of a national daily will have viewed 400 images by midday, so bear this in mind if you are targeting the nationals; the competition is fierce and you need a really good photo that is relevant and topical if you are to make it here.

NEWS RELEASE DISTRIBUTION LIST

Title of release: _____

_____

Date of issue: _____

Method of issue:

❏ Mail_____1st/2nd class   ❏ Fax_____   ❏ Courier_____

Issued to:

_____

_____

_____

_____

_____

_____

_____

_____

_____

_____

_____

_____

_____

_____

_____

_____

_____

_____

_____

_____

_____

_____

NEWS RELEASE CLEARANCE FORM

To:_____ Date:_____

The attached news release has been sent to you for comment and clearance.

Please respond with your comments by_____am/pm on_____

Title of release: _____

_____

Proposed date for issue: _____

Method of issue:

❑ Mail_____1st/2nd class   ❑ Fax_____   ❑ Courier_____

For issue to:

_____

_____

_____

_____

_____

_____

_____

_____

_____

_____

_____

_____

Circulated for comment to:_____

_____

Return comments to Sheena Singh

For events that are particularly photogenic, or more likely to make a photostory than a straight story without pictures, arrange a photocall. Send out a media invitation to picture desks (and TV), headed PHOTOCALL. Explain briefly what you are planning, and invite them to turn up at a certain time to film or photograph it. Set out your invitation like the example included in this book.

A WHO'S WHO OF NEWSPAPER STAFF

As with most organisations, a newspaper has a structure and it is useful to have a basic understanding of what it is and who does what within it.

Journalist/Reporter

There are specialist reporters or correspondents (such as housing, health and local government correspondents) and general reporters who have to write about a very wide range of issues but who may specialise in none.

Chief Reporter

As the name suggests, the chief reporter is more senior than other reporters and generally gets the best and most interesting assignments. They are usually more experienced than other reporters on the paper.

News Editor

The news editor selects the news, decides where in the paper it will appear, and assigns reporters to follow up particular stories.

Sub Editor

Cutting stories to fit the space and headline-writing are two of the main responsibilities of the sub. Sub editors can be brutal, shortening stories by chopping the final paragraph and creating a rather sudden ending!

Editor

As everyone knows, this is the top job on a newspaper. On larger newspapers it is generally a management job rather than a hands-on writing position, although the editor often writes a leader or comment column. On small papers and free papers, the editor can also be a reporter of sorts. Ultimately the editor is responsible for the content, tone and style of a newspaper.

WORK HARD AT RELATIONSHIPS

In many ways being a journalist is rather a lonely job. You dash around town meeting lots of people, but a fair amount of time is spent in unfamiliar rooms with unknown people. That's why journalists appreciate it when someone is there to meet them, greet them, give them a cup of coffee and introduce them to the people they need to talk to. This is all part of building up a good relationship with journalists. You need to be helpful and professional, always to meet their deadlines, and available to keep them informed of newsworthy developments. Do this and they will soon come to realise that you are an important source of information. Hopefully the closer you get, the more you will be able to trust them not to misrepresent you. You need each other, so aim for a reciprocal relationship and you will both gain.

Reporters keep a contacts book and refer to it when they need a comment on a particular issue. If you are viewed as especially helpful by a reporter, they will favour you over another spokesperson, thus giving you the chance to get valuable publicity and to be seen as an authority in your field. So when reporters start ringing you out of the blue for comment on an issue, or because they have a gap in the paper and wonder if you can help them fill it, you know that you have achieved that all-important relationship.

MAKING NEWS – HERE'S HOW!

Charities and voluntary organisations do scores of newsworthy things as part of their everyday work, and much of this is never publicised, either because no one thinks to do so, or because no one knows how to. Get into the habit of sending a release to your local papers whenever you have anything to say. If you cannot afford an in-house PR officer, give someone responsibility for PR and make sure that they are informed about what is happening in your organisation, and geared up to issue releases as necessary.

No organisation can be totally un-newsworthy. If a widget factory can get coverage, so can you. Here are just a few of the many things you probably already do that are worth publicising:

- **Landmarks** – such as your 1,000th new supporter, your first £100 raised, or your 3,000th signature on a petition

- **Anniversaries** – such as your 10th birthday

- **New services** – or extensions of your service to new client groups

- **Appointments** – announce the appointment of new members of staff

- **Publications** – such as new leaflets or your annual report

> **TRUE STORY**
>
> A journalist writing a piece about Sunday trading contacted her local supermarket for its weekend opening hours. She was told that they were not allowed to talk to the media and that all calls must be directed to the press office at head office. "But I only want to know if you're open on Sunday," said the exasperated reporter. "You are, presumably, allowed to talk to the public," she asked. When the reply was affirmative, so said "OK then, I'm a member of the public. Are you open on Sunday?" She finally got the answer she was looking for, and could have been spared a great deal of hassle and frustration had the supermarket staff been a little less rigid.

> **TIP**
>
> *Never announce two things at the same time. You'll get twice as much media attention if you leave a gap between, and make two separate announcements.*

■ **Research and surveys** – both when you commission it and when the findings are ready

■ **New premises** – or alterations to your premises, to introduce new facilities or to make them more accessible

■ **Predictions** – what you believe future trends in your field will be

■ **Announcements** – new plans or extra funding, for example

■ **Issues** – homelessness, third world issues, poverty, drug abuse etc.

■ **Investment** – new investment or funding

■ **Events** – open days, fundraising activities, jumble sales, exhibitions etc.

■ **Topical comment** – Christmas homelessness, winter heating bills, lack of playscheme facilities in the summer holidays etc.

■ **Action** – for example, 'The Dunsmyre Women's Group is calling for more and better breast feeding facilities in shops, restaurants and civic buildings in the town...' or 'Maychapel Animal Rights Campaign is calling for immediate action to be taken to stop laboratory testing on live animals ...'

Some organisations are concerned that in promoting their successes, there is a risk that they will create too rosy a picture, detracting attention from the problems they are trying to tackle, such as homelessness or poverty. Remember that news releases can also be used to provide comment, and to debate issues, so you need not fear that you must only release good news. Always ensure that your comment or opinion has a focus or is in some way topical. It must have a storyline if a reporter is to use it. (For more information on how to develop a storyline, see the section later in this chapter.)

Why not have PR down as an item at every staff meeting or management group meeting, so that you get into the habit of thinking about what you are doing, how newsworthy it is, and whether it could be publicised by a news release? You can then get your designated PR person to take the necessary action.

TIP

If your charity is large enough or specialised enough, you can try to become known experts in your field, so that the media contact you when they are looking for spokespeople on your subject. Put together a list of people in your organisation who are expert in their subject, include their home telephone number, and send your list to newsrooms. Set it out something like this:

SPOKESPEOPLE ON CHILDREN'S WELFARE
Staff from the charity Children First are happy to be contacted at our office or at home for information, comment or quotes on the following areas:

Dr. Mary Claire – child psychology, the effects of TV and video games on children, truancy and the reasons for it, bullying. Tel. 77601 (home)

Mike Smith – drug abuse amongst youngsters, peer group pressure. Tel. 92340 (home)

Asuk Uddin – child sex abuse, physical abuse, help available for children. Tel. 87231 (home)

Alternatively, call our Press Officer, Kate Sanditch, on 667541 (office) or 67783 (home).

TURN THE DULL INTO THE DAZZLING

If you have some news, turn it into a news release following the guidelines in this book. But do make sure that what you send is interesting and has some genuine news value. If you don't, your release will end up in the bin whatever you do to it – and that outcome is a waste of everyone's time. A journalist once told me that if you want the media to clamber over you for your story, the only way is for you to have on offer a photograph of Lord Lucan riding Shergar! The reality is that you will never have news this sensational, and you will have to find some way of giving your story an angle and making it more dazzling or more newsworthy.

You must ensure that you capture the news editor's attention in the first paragraph; if you don't, they will not bother to read on. You must also include all the relevant information early on in your release, by covering 'The Five Ws' (see box, right). These stand for: Who, What, When, Where, Why.

It is important that your release includes all this information fairly early on; the textbooks will tell you that it should come in the first sentence, but don't be too rigid about this, as it can make for a boring release. Instead you should aim for something newsworthy in the first paragraph, and continue with the Five Ws in the second one.

> **THE FIVE Ws**
>
> **W** ho – who will be doing it?
>
> **W** hat – what will they be doing?
>
> **W** hen – when will they be doing it?
>
> **W** here – where will they be doing it?
>
> **W** hy – why will they be doing it?

Here's an example of an opening paragraph that rigidly follows the Five Ws formula:

> Jenny James, Director of Ambletown Play Initiative, will be cutting a ribbon to mark the opening of their latest children's playscheme in Cambridge Street at 11am on Tuesday.

It has all the facts, but it's boring. How can you turn a dull story like this into a more exciting one? By thinking about the story and its relevance to users and local people. Where's the human interest for ordinary newspaper readers? The same story, turned on its head, would read:

> The hassle of school holidays for working parents has now been removed, in Ambletown at least, thanks to the Ambletown Play Initiative, which opens its newest playscheme in Cambridge Street today (Tuesday).
>
> It will be officially opened by Jenny James, with the help of a dozen face-painted children.......

The story leads with an angle that explains what the initiative will mean for its users – parents. This is of more interest than the fact that a senior official is going to cut a ribbon and declare the playscheme open. By using face-painted children, a photo-opportunity is also created.

So remember to lead with a newsworthy angle. To find your angle, ask yourself: Is what we are doing the biggest? Is it a first? Is it special in some way? What will it mean for our users or supporters? What will it mean for the town? Is there a more interesting angle? Is there something different or unique about it? Is it controversial? Are we breaking new ground in doing this?

Finding a more interesting angle is crucial to making your release newsworthy, as the real life example in the box on the left shows.

On page 46 you can see some more examples of news angles – this time fictitious – of how to do it (and how not to do it):

These news release opening paragraphs show how to find the news angle and to capture the attention of the news editor. Never bury a good story in the final paragraph. If you do, it will certainly rest in peace. On page 48 is an example of a complete news release, illustrating layout as well as presenting an interesting storyline.

Another useful device for introductory paragraphs is to use statistics, but to present them in a thought-provoking way. For example, don't write "3,000 people die every year from..." Write instead "The equivalent of a jumbo jet crashing every month..." Or instead of "Each year over 15 million people contract gumbar disease..." say "Every two seconds someone in Britain contracts..."

On the sample release, you will see that a *'Notes to editors'* has been included. This is where you include background information that is useful or interesting, but not vital to the story. It helps keep your release shorter, but ensures that you don't leave out something that could be useful to the reporter. One of the notes to editors contains additional information about the Anthorpe Unemployment Project. You might find it useful to include a similar note about your own organisation, dropping it once you are sure that your local papers know who you are and what you do.

✗ **WRONG**

The Dunpool Drop-in Centre has conducted a survey of its 2,500 users and the findings are being published today.

✓ **RIGHT**

Up to 95 per cent of people using the Dunpool Drop-in Centre may be caught in a poverty trap, according to the findings of a survey published today.

✗ **WRONG**

Supporters of the Mayor Port Dogs' Home held a flag day last week and collected nearly £200.

✓ **RIGHT**

Over 100 dogs will now get a Christmas dinner thanks to the generosity of local people, who donated nearly £200 when supporters of the Mayor Port Dogs' Home held their annual flag day last week.

✗ **WRONG**

Yesterday the Catterston Poverty Action Group held its annual general meeting, and guest of honour was local MP Doreen Anderson.

✓ **RIGHT**

The impact of poverty in Catterston could easily be reduced, if funding to the town's Poverty Action Group were to be doubled. That is the view of local MP Doreen Anderson, who last night addressed over 100 guests at the Group's AGM.

✗ **WRONG**

The Doverstone Well Woman Campaign today published its annual report for 1995, a 25 page document with sections on healthy eating, women's health problems, and an account of the year's activities.

✓ **RIGHT**

During 1995 the Doverstone Well Woman Campaign made a major contribution to improving the health of women in the county, by providing help and advice to over 2,000 women on health screening, diet and exercise.

Anthorpe Unemployment Project

10 High Street, Anthorpe. Tel. 01993 123456

NEWS RELEASE

For immediate use
Thursday, November 10 1998

NEW LIFE FOR FORMER BREWERY

The old brewery in Towngate Street, Anthorpe, which has been derelict for nearly 20 years, is to be given a new lease of life. Anthorpe Unemployment Project plans to turn it into a drop-in centre for unemployed youngsters in the town.

Facilities at the new centre will include a café, video room and snooker tables. There will also be a 'job club' office, where people will be able to prepare CVs and application letters using a word processor. Work on the £100,000 redevelopment of the brewery will begin in December, and the centre will open in February.

Aileen Anstruther, Director of Anthorpe Unemployment Project, said: "The brewery is an eyesore at the moment. Our redevelopment will provide a much-needed facility for unemployed young people, as well as restoring an architecturally and historically important building to its former glory".

Young people aged from 16 to 21 will be able to use the facilities free of charge.

ends

Notes to editors:

1. £90,000 of the finance for the development has been provided by the district council, and the balance came from fundraising activities.

2. The Anthorpe Unemployment Project has been running for two years, and during that time it has helped over 400 youngsters in the town to get permanent jobs.

For further information contact:

Aileen Anstruther, Director	Andrew Granton, Chair
Day 01993 12345	Day 01993 88904
Evening 01993 33456	Evening 01993 56545

FIVE TIPS FOR GREATER SUCCESS

There are five ways in which you can increase, sometimes quite dramatically, your chances of success in attracting media attention.

1. If you can, time your events or releases for a Sunday, as little news happens then. You might have noticed how Monday's papers are often quite thin, and this is why. Newspapers have staff working on Sundays in order to produce Monday's paper, although the day tends to be a fairly quiet one in the newsroom.

2. Along the same lines, plan events or releases for slack times such as the period between Christmas and New Year, or bank holidays. By having less to compete with, you increase your chances of success.

3. When dealing with weekly or monthly papers, find out what day they go to press, for the day following press day is a flat one, compared to the business of the day before. This can be the best time to make contact, for it is the least busy period, and it is when reporters are thinking about material for the next issue.

4. Remember the Press Association. They look over the news releases they are sent, and those that merit it are edited and issued as items which are available to newsrooms via telex and computer links. If the Press Association think your release is of interest, the chances are that it will be picked up by a national newspaper too, even if it just makes one or two paragraphs. (Look in newspapers for small news items which say 'PA' at the end. This means that they were issued by the Press Association.) The Press Association have offices in various cities, so find out the address of the one nearest you by looking in Yellow Pages under 'News and Photo Agencies'.

5. Avoid Thursdays and Fridays if you can, for Thursday tends to be a major parliamentary day and it's also the time when big court cases are coming to an end. Friday is a bad day for an event because it will be covered in Saturday's paper, which has fewer news pages and is taken up with entertainment information, TV listings etc.

HAVE A GO YOURSELF

Now that you know all the DOs and DON'Ts about news releases, you can put your knowledge into practice. Start by rewriting the news release in the exercise overleaf, your aim being to make it more likely to be used by a local newspaper. While doing this, try to remember what you have read in this chapter.

NEWS RELEASE EXERCISE

Embargo. Not for use until
Wednesday, July 27 1999

SMOKING BAN CALLED FOR

Smoking and smoking-related illnesses kill thousands of people every year across the country. This is due to the scores of different carcinogens to be found in tobacco smoke. In addition to the health problems caused, smoking also makes hair and clothes smell, and is generally anti-social.

That is why the Littleton Anti-smoking Campaign (LASC) thinks smoking should be banned in all shops, restaurants, theatres and cinemas in the town centre, in order to protect the rights of people who do not wish to smoke.

LASC's Campaign Manager, Humphrey Lewis, said: "It's outrageous that these filthy smokers should blow their disgusting, foul and dangerous smoke all over innocent people who have never harmed anyone in their lives. Smoking must be banned now, and until it is, our members will be boycotting town centre premises which allow smoking."

ends

For further information contact:

Humphrey Lewis
Campaign Manager
01961 67115 (office)

DISCUSSION

What was wrong with that release?

- The newsworthy bit – the boycott – is buried in the very last sentence

- The opening paragraph, which must catch a news editor's attention, has a national, not a local angle

- The quote makes the campaign group sound fanatical, unbalanced and unreasonable

- The release is not designed to win support

- An unnecessary embargo has been placed on the release

- There is no after hours contact number

So how should the release have looked? Compare yours to the one below.

For immediate use
Sunday, July 24 1999

LITTLETON PREMISES TO BE BOYCOTTED IN SMOKING BAN PLEA

Smoking should be banned in all town centre restaurants, shops, theatres and cinemas, according to the Littleton Anti-smoking Campaign, who are organising a boycott of premises which allow smoking.

Campaign Manager Humphrey Lewis said: "Non-smoking Littletonians are harmed each day by breathing in other people's tobacco smoke. Last year nearly 100 non-smokers in Littleton died of lung cancer from breathing in other people's smoke. We are calling our boycott to protect these people."

ends

For further information contact:

Humphrey Lewis	Jennifer Jenkins
Campaign Manager	Campaign Officer
01961 67115 (office)	01961 67115 (office)
or 01961 11212 (home)	or 01961 12577 (home)

DISCUSSION

What makes this one better?

- ■ It has a local angle right at the start of the release and in the headline

- ■ It has a quote that is thought-provoking, with local statistics, and is designed to win support

- ■ It contains no unnecessary information

- ■ There is a home contact number and a second contact person

VIDEO NEWS RELEASES

A video news release (VNR) is a news story produced on video to broadcast quality. Not surprisingly they are expensive, and generally they're the preserve of big companies, but pressure groups and national charities are making use of them for publicising particularly important issues or campaigns.

A basic VNR package, which includes production, UK distribution and a report on coverage obtained, costs between £5,000 and £15,000, so clearly they're not for everyone.

Like conventional paper news releases, they are sent out to TV newsrooms to be used as the producer sees fit. And like news releases, many are rejected, but those that make it onto the screens are presented as if the programme did the filming, carried out the interviews and so on. Viewers cannot tell the difference between a VNR and a report complied by the TV station's own news team.

VNRs originated in the United States in the 1980s and they reached our shores in the 1990s, with around 3,500 being made in this country each year. Broadcasters say that they don't like them, yet with increased pressure on news teams, VNRs do get used, as they are a cheap and easy way for broadcasters to get news. With the growth in satellite stations, there is a ready market for video news releases, although a charity would need to think carefully about whether satellite TV reaches their target audiences.

The housing charity Shelter used a VNR when it launched Home Truths in 1994, a campaign to prevent a housing Green Paper from becoming a white one. It resulted in 18 minutes 19 seconds of total coverage in 14 separate broadcasts, reaching an estimated 5.1 million people. To pay for that airtime would have cost £226,563.

The Health Education Authority used a VNR to publicise the long-term dangers of smoking during pregnancy. Their outlay of £10,000 resulted in coverage valued at £1 million, reaching an audience of 49 million through 28 news bulletins on the BBC, commercial TV, satellite TV and regional programmes.

If you are in the big league and interested in using VNRs, there are a number of companies specialising in it, though they are mainly London-based. Always approach more than one company, ask to see examples of their work, and take up references. Check that their staff have TV experience and an understanding of the requirements of news producers. Check also about their TV contacts and their distribution lists. You might find it illuminating to ask how many clients they turn away; some companies will take you on so long as you can afford their fee, while the better ones will advise you against producing a VNR if they believe that your story is not newsworthy enough. Bear in mind, though, that if your story is very newsworthy, you might not need to produce a VNR at all!

MEDIA INVITATIONS

From high-tech to low-tech and the humble but effective media invitation. It is best to send an invitation out about a week before your event. Make sure you include a paragraph explaining the purpose of the event and describing what will happen at it, and check that you have listed all the necessary information, such as start times, venue and so on. If the venue is difficult to find, include a simple map and directions. If you can, get a central venue, one that is easy to get to, and arrange parking for the media – this is essential for film crews, who will have lots of heavy equipment.

Media invitations serve to attract reporters to your event, but they should not take the place of a news release, which has quite a different purpose. See sample invitation overleaf.

When a news desk receives an invitation, the news editor will make a decision about the newsworthiness of your event. If it looks interesting, it will be entered into the diary and a reporter sent along. Events with picture potential will be passed to the picture editor, who will arrange for a photographer to attend. Boring events will not be attended, but don't assume your event was boring just because no media turned up. It could be that they were short-staffed that day, or that there was a more important event on at the same time.

Keep a list of who you invited, and don't hesitate to ring to see if they are coming. If they can't make it, offer to send the reporter a news release – but consider carefully when you will send it. If your release is delivered before your event takes place, it could put the reporter off coming by giving them the opportunity to cover the story based only on your release. On the other hand, it could persuade them that they really must be at your event!

Anthorpe Unemployment Project

10 High Street, Anthorpe. Tel. 01993 123456

FOR OPERATIONAL USE ONLY: NOT FOR PUBLICATION OR BROADCAST

INVITATION TO NEWS AND PICTURE EDITORS

TV BARMAID BET GILROY TO OPEN FORMER BREWERY DROP-IN CENTRE

Coronation Street's most famous barmaid, Bet Gilroy, will be in Anthorpe next week to officially open Anthorpe Unemployment Project's new drop-in centre, at the former brewery in Towngate Street.

She will crack open a magnum of champagne with unemployed teenagers James Dillon and Mairi MacIntosh, who will use the centre's facilities to help themselves get a job.

You are invited to send a representative

Time:	10.30am
Date:	Thursday, February 2 1999
Venue:	The Old Brewery, Towngate Street, Anthorpe

For further information contact:

Aileen Anstruther, Director
Day: 01993 12345
Evening: 01993 33456

Make sure you assign someone the task of meeting the media at the event, and checking on their needs. If you are helpful to reporters and photographers, they are more likely to be well-disposed towards your organisation, and to attend future events, but if you regard them as an irritation, you would be better off not inviting them at all.

The other main things you need to know about if you are to have a good relationship with the media are:

FEATURES

If you have ideas for features, get in touch with your newspaper. The Features Editor will be on the lookout for material and will welcome contact from you with a possible feature. It's best to start by writing a brief letter outlining your idea. Follow this up a week later with a call to assess interest.

If you can't get a feature dedicated to your cause or to the work of your charity, why not try for a mention in someone else's feature? Many trade and professional publications produce regular features, and they put together features lists, which set out what subjects they will be covering and when. You can get these simply by ringing the publication and asking for one. (There are services you can subscribe to which tell you about forthcoming features, though they are expensive. The best known of these is Advance, who will also do a personalised editorial feature research for you on specific topics. Its publishers, Themetree Limited, also produce a comprehensive guide to forthcoming conferences and exhibitions in the UK and Europe. They can be contacted on 01296 28585.)

Once you find a feature that is relevant to your work, write to the Features Editor explaining how you can help/contribute, perhaps by supplying some facts and figures, being interviewed, or sending the reporter some useful background material. You might end up getting valuable publicity, but even if you don't, you will have made a useful contact as well as making yourself known to the publication. They might well get back to you in the future.

If you have in mind a topical feature, remember that magazines have a very long lead-in time, often more than three months. So if your proposed feature is a Christmas one, you'll need to make your approach no later than August, as that's when they will be putting the magazine together.

PRESS CONFERENCES

Press conferences are often called 'news conferences' these days because they are aimed at the broadcast media as well as newspapers. Don't have them unless you have something really important to say. They are a lot of hard work to organise, and the media won't thank you for dragging them out to hear some news that does not merit the effort they have made. Journalists claim that up to nine out of ten news conferences they attend are a waste of their time, either because there is no newsworthy story on offer, or because they could get the same information in a news release, thereby saving themselves the hassle of leaving their desk.

So if you are considering holding a news conference, ask yourself "Would a release be just as effective?" If the answer is "Yes", send one and save everyone a lot of unnecessary effort.

If you are certain that a news conference is necessary, be realistic about who will attend. Don't expect the sort of attendance that you see on TV, where there are photographers' flashguns going off, packed rooms full of reporters, and TV microphones everywhere. Even if you get several national newspapers plus radio and television – which is unlikely – you will only have around half a dozen people!

The golden rule for news conferences is to start (and end) on time. Journalists are busy people, under pressure and working to tight deadlines. They have better things to do than sit around waiting for you to get started (or finished!). Say what you have to say, keep it to a minimum, and then shut up. If there's something you haven't covered, you can be sure that a reporter will ask you about it.

If your story is worthy of a news conference, points to bear in mind are:

- **TIMING:** The ideal time is around 11am. This allows TV and evening papers to cover the event, as well as the dailies. It also enables radio to attend and to get back in time to broadcast your news on the lunchtime bulletin.

- **SIGNING IN:** Take a note of who attended by asking attendees to sign a guest book. It's useful if you want to monitor coverage or fax releases to those who could not make it.

- **NAMES:** Speakers at the top table should have name plates. Issue guests with name badges.

- **FACILITIES:** Check your venue for power points for TV crews to use and make sure there's a quiet side room for radio interviews to take place.

Sometimes radio or TV reporters cannot attend at the time you have scheduled, and they might ring to ask you if they can do an early interview; perhaps that morning, or even the day before. Try to be as helpful as you can at accommodating this, as ultimately it's your charity that will benefit from the coverage.

As with other events to which you are inviting TV and radio, make parking available if you can, try to find a central venue, and send maps if your venue is at all off the beaten track.

PRESS PACKS

A press pack, sometimes known as a press kit, is simply an A4 wallet or folder containing a news release or releases and background briefing material such as facts and figures, leaflets about your organisation, and anything else of interest, plus relevant captioned photographs and illustrations. Use press packs to hand out to the media at events and press conferences.

OFF THE RECORD

And finally to 'off the record'. The golden rule is never to tell a journalist anything unless you are willing for it to be reported. There are occasions when off the record briefings are useful, and very experienced PR practitioners can use them skilfully, but if you are fairly new to the game they are unnecessary and best avoided.

We have concentrated so far on newspapers, because they will be your main source of coverage, but don't overlook radio and television for important stories.

RADIO AND TELEVISION

Television can be difficult to get onto, though do send releases to TV news if it's a big story. Local radio is easier to get airtime on, although it is becoming harder as stations reduce their staff. If radio or TV wish to cover your story, they will:

- invite you into the studio for a live or recorded interview or

- do a recorded or live interview down the telephone (radio only) or

- do their own news report based on your release, possibly following a brief, informal chat with you on the telephone, or

- send a reporter to you

Sometimes you will get asked onto TV or radio as a direct result of your news release. Or you may get a call out of the blue, because a researcher is looking for an expert to provide comment or opinion, and you have been recommended, or are already known to them. Or you could get on air through choice – by calling a phone-in programme, for example.

Another way of getting on TV is to find out what programmes are being made and to try and influence the producers. Finding out about programmes in the pipeline is too big a job for any charity to take on, for there are over 1,000 independent

> **TIP**
>
> *Phone-in programmes on radio and TV are a good and incredibly easy way of getting coverage regionally or even nationally. It's so simple – just pick up the phone, dial the number, chat to the researcher (you will never end up on air direct) and then you may be selected to go on the airwaves. It's your ideal chance to publicise a cause.*

production companies, in addition to the BBC and ITV. The only feasible way of keeping up to date is to subscribe to a service that will tell you who is making what and when. A publication called Programme News (call 0171 793 8220 for details) provides early warning of programmes in production or currently being planned. It gives a brief synopsis of the content, contact, and details of support the programme makers would welcome. The annual subscription is well under £200, so consider clubbing together with other local charities and sharing a subscription.

If your organisation is invited onto radio or TV, ask if the interview will be live or recorded and find out who else will be appearing. Always pick the best spokesperson – who may not be the director or chairperson – and aim for someone who speaks articulately and succinctly, and who you believe will come across well with the audience that particular programme is likely to attract. If you are asked to send your director, but you know that they will be hopeless, say so (tactfully) and suggest that you send a better spokesperson instead.

Using a Self-Operate Studio

When it comes to radio programmes, whether you are doing an interview live or recorded, you may come across a self-operate studio. You will have to use one of these if your contribution is coming from one city and the programme is being broadcast from another. Essentially a 'self-op' is a small studio containing a table, chair, microphone, small control panel and telephone. You will be called on the phone by the programme-maker, who will explain what happens next and which buttons to press. It can be nerve-wracking sitting alone in the studio waiting for the phone to ring, but keep calm and you'll do OK.

Looking the part

Think carefully about what to wear for a TV appearance. Go for something that makes you feel comfortable and confident and that is suitable for the occasion. Whether it's right or wrong, you will be judged by how you look and dress, so give yourself a head start by looking the part.

TIP

When you are doing an interview, take a deep breath, then relax! If you don't, the listener or viewer will pick up your nervousness. Forget the thousands (or millions!) of people listening and watching, and just concentrate on the interviewer. Imagine it's just the two of you, and you will be less nervous. Don't look at the camera, look at the interviewer.

Women should not wear large, dangly earrings that will distract viewers, or glinty jewellery that will catch the light too much. Never wear strapless dresses, or you will appear to be naked in head and shoulders shots!

Men should avoid shirts and ties where the stripes are too close together, as this comes out badly on TV. So do jackets with very small checks. Make sure your socks are long enough to cover your hairy ankles!

Never fidget or fiddle with your hair or clothing, as this is really irritating for viewers. And don't swivel about on your chair, rock to and fro or wave your hands in a manic way. Pointing you finger on TV is definitely a no-no; you'll look aggressive and will lose the support of viewers.

> **TIP**
>
> *If you are doing a radio interview and you need notes, don't have them on paper, as the rustling will be picked up by the microphone. Write your prompts on small pieces of card instead.*

Preparation is all important. Know what you want to say (and what you are not willing to discuss) and be familiar with all the facts and figures, but don't quote too many statistics on air – it's a real turn-off for listeners. If you have time, do a trial run with a colleague beforehand, and tape-record it. That way you will be made aware of any irritating verbal mannerisms such as "you know" and "well, ummmm...", and you can then try to avoid them.

Speak clearly, in plain language, and try not to speak too fast. Never use jargon.

Most of the time an interviewer will not be trying to catch you out. They are as keen as you are for the interview to go smoothly; if it runs badly, it will not reflect well on them. If they ask a strange-sounding question, it's simply to get you to speak, so don't be worried. Their aim is to get you relaxed and talking, not tongue-tied.

Generally you will get a chance to have an informal chat with the interviewer or researcher before you go on air. They might ask you some questions, or get you to fill them in on the background to the story. At this stage you can ask questions too, if there is anything you are unsure about. Some people like to know in advance what questions they will be asked, although many interviewers are reluctant to reveal them. This is simply because they fear that you will rehearse the answers and come across on air in a stilted and unnatural way.

The biggest problem you will face on radio and television is lack of time. Most TV interviews last an average of two minutes twenty-four seconds, up to half of which is taken up with the interviewer talking. That leaves very little time for you, so be clear from the outset on the main points you want to get across, and stick to these. You should certainly not try to make more than three points. Ensure they are extremely simple, as you will be addressing an uninformed audience (via, in all probability, an uninformed interviewer).

Trying to get your points across can be difficult because the interviewer may not ask you the right questions. It's up to you to turn questions around to enable you to get your points across. For example, if you want to get the following three points over:

■ we want a by-pass for the village, to stop heavy lorries thundering through

■ we regard the lorries as a danger to the public

■ the roads in the village were not designed for vehicles of this size and weight

This is how you do it:

Interviewer: Surely you cannot justify the enormous cost of building a by-pass? Some would say you are being selfish to expect the public purse to pay for a major road to be built just so that you can prune your roses in peace and quiet.

Campaigner: We're campaigning on a public safety issue. Children and pensioners in our village are in daily danger from lorries that present a hazard to pedestrians, other road users and to property.

Interviewer: That's all very well but what about the tens of thousands of pounds needed for a by-pass? Would that public money not be better spent on more teachers or nurses?

Campaigner: You can't put a price on human life or human history. Our village needs a by-pass to protect its people, including young children, and its irreplaceable historic buildings. The road through our village was designed for horses and carts, not ten-ton articulated lorries.

Never get drawn into answering questions that will detract from the main points you want to get across.

CONTROVERSIAL ISSUES

Sometimes charities, and especially pressure groups, are interviewed about quite controversial issues. If that's what you have been asked to speak about, you should bear the following in mind:

■ The aim of the interview will be to create interesting and exciting television or radio, so make sure you are not being set up. Find out in advance who else will be appearing and then decide whether or not you want to do the interview

■ Be clear about what you are not willing to say, but never say "No comment": find another way of avoiding a difficult question. Practice this before the interview, and watch news and current affairs programmes to see how the experts – politicians – avoid tricky questions without loss of face

■ Don't let the interviewer make you lose your temper – always keep calm, whatever you are accused of, but do make sure that you firmly but politely rebut anything that is incorrect or untrue. If you lose your temper, you will lose the argument, because the viewer or listener will side with the interviewer and you will come across as aggressive and unprofessional

■ Be as positive as you can be

■ Always be prepared to consider *not* doing the interview, if you believe that it will do more harm than good. You don't have to accept an invitation – be clear on what you want to get out of it

MEDIA MONITORING AND EVALUATION

If you deal with the media quite a lot, you will probably benefit from keeping a media log, which records any dealings you have with reporters. It is useful to do this, as it helps you build up a picture of media interest in your charity and enables you to monitor your media coverage. There is a sample media enquiry form in this book.

The idea of an enquiry form is that it ensures that enquiries from the media are recorded properly, dealt with efficiently, and that a record exists of any response made. If you are misquoted, you have a copy on file as evidence.

Develop your own monitoring form based on the one in this book, and make sure that supplies are available at reception and with anyone who might have to take calls from the media. Completed forms should be filed in a ring binder.

When it comes to monitoring your coverage, you can – if you have the money – use a press cuttings service. This is a company which specialises in reading practically every publication – from the national press to obscure publications such as Pig World and Pigeon Racers' Gazette. Press clippings agencies read trade and technical press, consumer publications, and other specialist magazines, as well as national, local and regional papers. They then cut out all articles which refer to your organisation and send them to you with a note of where and when they appeared.

If you use an agency, they will charge you a monthly reading fee (around £100 will cover you for all publications), and on top of that you need to pay a set price for each cutting (usually in the region of 80p). All of this can work out very expensive, so it only makes sense if you have a really big campaign on and monitoring is vital. (Try to negotiate a special deal – never accept the first price you are quoted.) Even then, it's often possible to do it yourself, unless you are sending material to a very large number of publications.

It's also possible to get verbatim transcripts of radio and television interviews from monitoring companies, although again it's very expensive (around £40 for a transcript of an interview lasting up to two minutes). You can also get copies of interviews on video (around £60) or cassette tape (around £30). Always ask the price before using one of these companies, or you could be in for a shock when you get the invoice.

Requesting something for urgent delivery (e.g. the same day or overnight) adds a premium of up to 50%. There is no need to subscribe to these companies to use the service, although if you are a subscriber, they will ring you up to let you know about mentions; you don't need to call them.

If you monitor your coverage, you should also seek to evaluate it. One of the sample forms in this book is an evaluation form, aimed to help you assess whether the coverage you received was helpful or not. An unsophisticated approach to press evaluation (still used by many) is simply to measure the column inches of coverage you receive, but this tells you nothing of the quality of the coverage. The evaluation form in this book helps you to assess whether media coverage, including broadcast coverage,

---

MEDIA ENQUIRY FORM

Name of reporter_____

Publication/TV or radio programme_____

Telephone number_____

Call received on (date)_____at (time)_____am/pm

Message taken by_____

Nature of enquiry:

Deadline_____

Response:

Issued by_____

Date and time_____

MEDIA EVALUATION

Publication/programme:_____

Date:_____

Subject:_____

Did the coverage convey any of the key messages we wanted to promote? If so, which ones?

_____

_____

_____

_____

_____

_____

Did it get anything wrong? If so, was the error(s) damaging?

_____

_____

_____

_____

_____

_____

Was the news item favourable/helpful, unhelpful/damaging or neutral? In what way?

_____

_____

_____

_____

_____

_____

was a help or a hindrance, and whether it conveyed the messages you hoped it would. You can develop your own form based on the one here, adding questions relevant to your own organisation. For example, you might attempt to measure whether increased media coverage has led to an increase in donations or requests for your publications.

Media evaluation is increasingly becoming a science. It is now possible to get evaluation software that will help you assess the value of your press coverage, both in financial terms and in terms of its effect on your image. The software will produce all sorts of fantastic graphs and charts that will show you how much the coverage would have cost had you had to pay for it, whether it has communicated the key messages, and whether the editorial was in a prominent position in the publication.

Evaluation is more important than many organisations, including some very large ones, realise. It is pointless issuing releases and trying to attract coverage if you do not stop to assess whether your releases are doing any good. If they only result in bad coverage, or no coverage at all, perhaps you are wasting your time.

KEEPING YOUR HEAD IN A CRISIS

The day comes for most charities when they have to deal with a crisis. Through no fault of your own you may receive bad publicity, and dealing with it promptly and efficiently can help you preserve and sometimes enhance the good image you have worked hard to establish.

There is considerable scope for charities to get bad coverage. A user might complain about the service, for example, or one of your staff might make off with fundraising money. It could even be that a planned project is causing controversy, perhaps because it is for drug users, ex-offenders or another group which the public and media feel unsympathetic about.

If something happens that results in bad coverage, or that you fear might result in negative press, take the following steps immediately:

The Crisis Action Guide

1. Don't panic. Remain calm and keep a sense of perspective

2. Brief staff who need to know about it

3. Don't forget to tell switchboard – they are the first line of contact for journalists, so they need to know how to react and who to put calls through to

4. Sit down and list the facts that you are prepared to release – share these with other staff who need to know, so you are all clear on what you can and can't say

5. Prepare a press statement (a short quote or outline of your views, see page 67/68) or news release to put forward your side of the story if necessary

6. Keep your own staff informed, to stop unhelpful gossip and rumour

Preparing in advance for a crisis, and having plans in place, will help you cope if/when the real thing happens. Identify potential crises and ensure that all relevant staff know what to do.

If a journalist gets hold of the controversial story and phones you up, play for time if you need to. You don't have to answer questions there and then. Simply make a note of the questions and promise to get back to the reporter in half an hour, explaining that you are in a meeting and that there are one or two facts you need to check. This will give you time to think about your response, and to discuss it with colleagues if necessary – but always make sure that you ring the reporter back within the agreed time.

You might find that reporters you have previously had a good relationship with become aggressive and pushy in pursuing their line of enquiry. Don't take it personally; they are paid to investigate stories. However hard they press you, remain polite and helpful, for you'll need their support again once everything blows over.

It might be that you were in the wrong, as an organisation, and often it is best to admit this openly, and to explain what you intend to do to rectify the situation.

Don't always be too forthcoming with information. First of all find out what the reporter knows – it might be much less than you think.

Finally, don't be surprised if you are phoned at home. Journalists are good at tracking people down. The same rules apply – take a note of the questions and then ring back once you have got your facts together. Make sure you have a note at your home of the home telephone numbers of relevant staff who you might need to talk to.

COMPLAINING ABOUT THE MEDIA

Sometimes the media will get it wrong and publish or broadcast inaccurate or damaging material. This may be done deliberately (though this is unlikely), carelessly (by not being thorough and checking their material) or innocently. There are a number of things you can do when the media makes a mistake. If it's something small (perhaps they spelt your name wrong or said that you employ 15 staff when you actually employ 18) it's best forgotten. It might matter to you, but it won't bother the reader or listener and you will appear petty if you complain.

Taking newspapers first, if the error is serious you should consider one of the following, depending on the circumstances:

■ an informal call to the editor to discuss the matter (always have in mind what outcome you would like)

■ a request that a correction, apology or full retraction is published

■ a request that a letter of complaint is published in the letters page

■ a deal whereby the paper agrees to do a more sympathetic article in a month or so (this will only work with local papers; nationals would never agree to this)

■ a suggestion that the reporter responsible visits your organisation for a couple of hours to find out more about what you do, so that errors will not occur in the future

■ a formal complaint to the Press Complaints Commission (this is the replacement body for the Press Council and can be contacted at 1 Salisbury Square, London EC4Y 8AE. Tel. 0171 353 1248.) It's best to do this only as a last resort, if you've been unable to rectify matters with the paper concerned. Write in with your complaint and all necessary material, such as a copy of the offending article, copies of correspondence between you and the paper etc.

A word of warning about complaints: before firing off an angry letter, stop and think. Will you damage a relationship that is important to you? Will you achieve anything by complaining? If so, what? Is it worth it? Is there a better way of dealing with it? Do you have the energy and time to go to the Press Complaints Commission?

If TV or radio make a mistake, contact the producer of the programme first. If that gets you nowhere, you can contact the broadcasting equivalent of the Press Complaints Commission, the Broadcasting Complaints Commission. They will only consider complaints which fall into at least one of the following categories:

■ unfair or unjust treatment in broadcast radio or TV programmes (including satellite and cable services)

■ unwarranted infringement of privacy in programmes or in their making

You should write to the Secretary of the Commission giving the title of the programme and the date and channel on which it was broadcast. Explain your complaint and supply any relevant information to back up your complaint. The Commission can be contacted at 35 and 37 Grosvenor Gardens, London SW1W 0BS (Tel. 0171 630 1966).

HAVE A GO YOURSELF

A small, local charity has just held its annual flag day, but one of the collectors has disappeared, taking the collection tin with him. The director gets a call that evening from the local paper. They ask for the name and address of the collector, an estimate of the amount that has gone missing, and a comment on the accusation (levelled by the newspaper) that the charity behaved unprofessionally and irresponsibly in allowing this to happen.

The director plays for time by promising to fax a statement to the newspaper first thing in the morning. She sends the following. Read through it, list what is wrong with it, then draft a better response.

PRESS STATEMENT EXERCISE

STATEMENT TO THE CORRINGTON COURIER FROM THE CORRINGTON HOME HELP CHARITY

Yesterday one of our collectors, David Smith, of 29 Acacia Avenue, disappeared with his collection tin, which we estimate to have contained around £55. We regard the incident as most regrettable, although we are pleased to say that this is only the second time that such an occurrence has happened in the last 30 years. The police have become involved and we are hopeful for the safe return of our money and the apprehension and detention of the culprit.

We have certainly not behaved irresponsibly or unprofessionally in allowing this to happen. Our collectors are vetted, but sadly this one slipped though the net. These things do happen from time to time, and there is nothing we, or any other charity, can do to prevent it. When money is involved, it is unfortunate that people who are less than honest can become involved with positions of responsibility, thus jeopardising the important work that charities do.

DISCUSSION

■ The first error the director makes is in answering all of the questions. Answer questions put to you if you think they will not damage your image or reputation, otherwise avoid them if you can. Often a newspaper will settle for a statement, and might not contact you again for further answers.

■ It was wrong of the director to reveal the name and address of the collector, who might well be innocent. This is a matter for the newspaper to follow up with the police.

- There was no need to state a sum of money, particularly as it was merely a guess.

- It was foolish of the director to mention that there had been a similar incident before. It does nothing for the public's confidence in the charity.

- It was a mistake for the director to try to address the accusation that the charity was unprofessional. In doing so, she put Corrington Home Help on the defensive and gave the paper an opportunity to publish a negative and damaging story along these lines...."Corrington charity denies a charge that it is unprofessional....."

- Saying that it is 'just one of those things', even if it is true, makes the charity appear complacent and unconcerned about the loss and the dishonesty.

- It sounds like a police report.

So what should she have said?

PRESS STATEMENT EXERCISE

STATEMENT TO THE CORRINGTON COURIER FROM THE CORRINGTON HOME HELP CHARITY

Yesterday one of our flag sellers failed to return his collecting tin and the matter is now being dealt with by the police. We would like to thank everyone who gave so generously during our collection, and to reassure them that we take every precaution to prevent incidents of the sort which occurred yesterday from happening.

Our annual flag day is very important for us, being our main fundraising event of the year, and the £2,000 that we raise in this way enables us to provide help and friendship to elderly people in Corrington. We are confident that the citizens of Corrington will continue to give generously to our charity, so that our valuable work in the town can continue.

DISCUSSION
This is better because:

- It is a more confident, positive, upbeat response.

- It stresses the important and valuable work of the charity, seizing an opportunity to promote the charity and deflect a bad story.

- It plays down the theft.

- It does not answer irrelevant or potentially damaging questions.

CHAPTER FOUR

EVENT MANAGEMENT

By events, we mean everything from seminars and conferences, through dinners and parties, to official occasions. Having a successful event is not difficult – but it does take time, planning and careful co-ordination. In this chapter we will show you how to make sure that your event is successful, and we kick off with three simple rules, which, if followed, will ensure your event runs smoothly.

1. Never assume – always check that you know who is doing what, and make sure that they know they are doing it too!

2. Have an event co-ordinator and ensure they are given the authority to get things done

3. Allow plenty of time – planning events always takes longer than you think

Even small events take a lot of time and planning to get right, and big ones can be a nightmare. Share the burden by setting up a planning committee to see the event through from initial conception to an after-the-event evaluation.

What event?

Call a meeting of the planning committee to decide on the type of event you want. It's better to involve more than one person in this process, as you're more likely to come up with creative and unusual ideas than if you sit down on your own to devise something. (Brainstorming can be a good way of listing the various options.) It's also a good idea to involve the planning committee in deciding on the event, because they are more likely to be committed to it if the idea is theirs rather than yours imposed on them.

> **TIP**
> *Try not to combine a social or 'thank you' event with a media event if you can help it, as it can lead to conflict. The media will attend your event for one reason – to get a story or photograph – and your guests will want something very different from it. If you do have to have dual purpose events involving the media, make sure that their needs can be catered for, preferably at the beginning, so they can attend, get their story, and disappear. This will leave your guests free to enjoy themselves.*

Boring or staid events are likely to be less well attended than something a bit different. There's no need to be totally wacky, just reasonably original. Things to avoid are ribbon-cutting ceremonies to mark an opening, presentation ceremonies of flowers, crystal and other unimaginative gifts, and dignitaries making sleep-inducing speeches!

Always ensure that your chosen event is appropriate. If you are a third world charity, holding a lavish banquet for your supporters might be considered insensitive. Timing is important, too. If you work in a Muslim community, don't hold a buffet in the middle of Ramadan. And make sure that your event is necessary. So many events take place simply because someone felt that it was a good idea, without ever stopping to think why. Never have an event for this reason. Always ask yourself: Why are we holding this event? What do we hope to achieve? Is there a less time-consuming or more cost-effective way?

Why are we doing this?

Being clear at the outset about what you want to achieve will help you in your planning, and you are far more likely to meet your objectives if you are explicit about what they are. Here are some examples of very different types of event, along with some possible objectives:

Event: A Lark in the Park

Objectives: To bring the community together

To give local kids a chance of some fun

To recruit new members for the community council

Event: Seminar on HIV/AIDS

Objectives: To raise awareness of the issue among health workers

To establish our organisation as an authority

To set up a network

To raise funds for our HIV work

To attract media coverage on the issue

Event: Exhibition at the Community Café

Objectives: To publicise our work to the wider public

To attract new supporters

Event: Annual general meeting

Objectives: To meet our legal requirements

To bring together supporters

To present the highlights of the year and to tell partner organisations about our plans for next year

To say thank you to everyone who has helped us during the last 12 months

Getting organised

Having decided on the event and set the objectives, it's time to get on with the planning. Start by listing **everything** you need to do in the form of a checklist. (If you are having a ceremonial cake cutting, someone must remember the knife. For a balloon release, someone is going to have to inflate them. It's these items of detail that are often overlooked, but which can undermine an event.) Assign each task to someone, and set a deadline. Circulate the checklist and get your event co-ordinator to keep a check on progress, and to remind staff about their tasks.

If you hold a lot of events, you might find it worthwhile setting up a checklist pro forma on your computer, to make planning even easier. This can be updated, and amended according to the event. You might also wish to computerise your guest lists according to event type – with one list for opening ceremonies, another for media events, and yet another for official functions.

On page 75 is a checklist of the type you might use yourself. It is worth doing your own checklist, because they save a lot of time and effort in the long run.

If your event requires equipment such as a video recorder or overhead projector, make sure it is working and that the presenter knows how to use it. Have contingency plans for equipment failure, such as spare bulbs and fuses. For talks, public meetings and similar events, always get the room set up well in advance, with the equipment in place and plugged in. By doing this, you will discover whether your leads are long enough, whether sockets are in the right place, whether blackout curtains are necessary and so on. This is especially important if you are hiring a venue with which you are unfamiliar.

Don't forget things like bluetack or pens for the flipchart. They might be small, minor bits of equipment, but it makes a very bad impression if they are overlooked, often ruining a seminar or meeting.

If you hope to attract the media to your event, be sure to fix the time to suit them and ensure that your venue and other arrangements are also suitable (see chapter on media relations).

The golden rule for successful events is to check and check again. Last minute events are the ones that are most likely to go wrong, so always allow plenty of time for planning and preparation. Try to identify possible events well in advance, and schedule them into your events calendar. Anniversaries are a good example of events that can easily be spotted in advance, as are regular happenings, such as AGMs. And finally, if you want your event to run smoothly, remember the Five Ps motto – Poor Planning Produces Paltry Performance!

Permission, insurance and accidents

Some events, or aspects of your event, will require permission from the police, local authority or another body. A balloon release, for example, needs permission as balloons released *en masse* interfere with airport radar. So does anything likely to upset traffic flow, such as a march or a carnival float. And if you need roads closed for a street party or outdoor event, you will need to arrange this well ahead.

Then there are licences to consider. If you plan to sell alcohol at your event you must have a Liquor Licence. Dancing and musical events will require an Entertainments Licence. There are various other licences you may require, depending on your plans, and laws and bye-laws to comply with. Contact the police and your local authority for details.

As if that's not enough to think about, don't forget insurance. Are you covered if someone has an accident? Although public liability insurance is not essential, it's a good idea to take it out as it is not expensive and gives peace of mind to event organisers.

For large public events you should get the St. John's Ambulance or Red Cross to attend, and budget for a donation to them in return for their help. Other considerations for public events are: Do you have sufficient stewards who are briefed on how to cope with accidents and crowd control? What about loos, parking, litter, food hygiene regulations, consultation with neighbours? What about contingency plans? These are essential for outdoor events, thanks to our unreliable climate, even in summer! (You can get rainfall insurance. Sadly it's not a weather guarantee, simply a policy to cover costs such as equipment hire if you are rained off. Contact an insurance broker for details.)

Choosing a venue

If your event is not on your premises, select a venue with care. Bear in mind the needs of those who will attend. They may need full disabled access, a vegetarian, Halal or Kosher meal, a smoke-free environment, a large room for a crèche, easy parking, good public transport links, an induction loop system for people with hearing aids....the list goes on.

The venue you choose should be appropriate for the type of event. Holding a jumble sale at the Ritz would be neither appropriate nor affordable. Hosting an expensive seminar in a seedy backstreet hotel would lead to complaints from your attendees.

For an event with a clear theme, try to select a venue to suit. So if you have raised money to save rare birds living in Nigeria's wetlands, ask the Nigerian High Commission if you can hold your event on their premises if you are in London.

If attendees are likely to be unfamiliar with your venue make sure that you have lots of signs and directional arrows to help them find their way to the right place. There's nothing more frustrating than getting lost trying to find the right building, or the right room within it.

Using a celebrity

If you want to pull in the crowds to your event, or you're after maximum media coverage, one sure way is to use a celebrity. Chances are that you will be unable to secure the services of a Hollywood megastar, top footballer or supermodel, even if you wanted to (unless you are one of the big national or international charities). Stars are choosy about what they do and they cost a lot of money. There are specialist agencies who will find you a famous face – for a price – but often it's inappropriate for a charity to spend money in this way.

Thankfully there are many actors and celebrities who are happy to do their bit for charity, though it's usually the larger charities that benefit from this generosity. It is difficult for small organisations with low profiles to persuade someone famous to support them, though it has been done. If you hope to enlist the support of a well known figure, start by selecting the right one to approach, bearing in mind that they are always being asked to do things for free and are unlikely to jump at the chance of helping you out, however worthy a cause you think you are. You have a greater chance of securing support if you restrict your approaches to those who have a known interest in your subject. TV presenter Anne Diamond, for example, supports a 'cot death' organisation; she lost her own child in this way and it's therefore something very personal to her. A mental health charity might choose to approach someone famous who has suffered from depression, such as John Cleese. A cat charity should obviously go for a famous cat-lover, such as Martin Lewis.

Don't send reams of paper as part of your initial approach, merely a to-the-point letter setting out what you do and why you need help. Specify whether you are looking for on-going support or a one-off appearance, and supply a small amount of background information such as a publicity leaflet or annual report. Remembering that most famous people have an ego of some sort, stress how pleased you would be if they agreed to support and how much your charity could benefit, though don't gush too much – they can recognise hyperbole! Next, sit back and be patient, as pestering will get you nowhere.

> **TRUE STORY**
>
> A woman opened a Scotch pie shop in Blackpool a few weeks before the Labour Party's conference in that town. Business was not brisk, so during the conference she sent a letter to John Prescott, Labour's Deputy Leader, asking him to give her shop a plug. He did, and she found herself in the national limelight when he dropped in for a pie with newspapers and TV crews in tow! So it's worth asking a famous face for a favour, even if you are not confident that they will respond, because you just never know!

Knowing how to get hold of stars can be a problem. If they are TV or radio people, send your letter to the programme they take part in, with a covering letter asking for it to be forwarded. For recording artists, write to the record company, for an author to the publisher, etc.

Timing

Give careful thought to the timing of your event. A public meeting at around 6.30pm will not attract people with young children. Day-time events rule out those with standard working hours. Be careful not to clash with other events being held locally, or even with favourite TV programmes if you are holding public meetings: Coronation Street is likely to win!

Time of the year is important too. A conference held in Edinburgh during the International Festival will attract premium rates from hotels and venues, assuming you can secure a booking. However, you might find that your conference is a sell out because everyone wants to come in order to sample the delights of the Festival after hours!

Briefing participants

Written briefs for anyone involved in your events are essential. If you are using a celebrity, inviting a guest speaker, or even just getting you chairperson along to say a few words, always issue a written brief. This should outline: why the event is taking place and what you hope to achieve; who else will be participating; what you expect of your speaker (e.g. a two minute introduction to an audience of around 100 using a PA system and speaking from a lectern on a podium); who will be in the audience; a programme of the event, along with a timetable; details of when to arrive and who to report to; practical information, e.g. parking. For a speaker who is unfamiliar with your organisation, include background information too.

The brief is the part of an event that is most often overlooked, perhaps because it is the least interesting to prepare. Yet without a good brief, your speakers will not know what they expect, they will have a poor view of your group and its ability to organise, and you will not get the best out of them. A well-briefed speaker is the one who makes the biggest impact on your audience.

The post mortem

Whether your event is a regular, such as your AGM, or a one-off, sit down afterwards and assess how it went. Did you achieve your objectives? If not, where did you go wrong? What lessons can you learn? Could you do it better next time? Evaluation is an important part of the learning process and even experienced events organisers have room for improvement.

EVENTS CHECKLIST

Name of event_____

Date of event_____

Update as at (date)_____

ACTIVITY	DEADLINE	ACTION BY WHOM	COMMENTS
decide on type of event			
set a date			
select speakers/participants			
check on their availability			
draw up programme and timetable			
check venue for suitability, e.g. access			
list props needed, e.g. red ribbon, giant scissors			
arrange for the supply of props			
draw up list of people to invite			
draw up media list			
book photographer and write confirming details of job			
write to speakers to confirm details and to brief them			
book caterers & don't forget special requirements (e.g. Kosher)			
get invitations printed			
draft and agree news release			
organise name badges			
organise the venue – top table, exhibition, signing-in book etc.			
mail invitations to guests			
mail invitations to media			
prepare press packs			
check on final numbers			
confirm final numbers with caterers			

CHAPTER FIVE

PUBLICATIONS

Even the very smallest charities produce publications – everything from leaflets and newsletters to annual reports and research reports. In this chapter you can pick up cost-effective tips on improving your publications and you can discover ways of making your material accessible to people with special needs. (The next chapter will show you how to write great copy, while Chapter 7 will explain how to get publications designed and printed.)

For many people, the only contact they will have with your organisation is through your publications, so it is important that they reflect the image you wish to convey. You can promote a positive image through careful choice of writing style, content and design. These three areas will be covered in chapters 5-7.

Before producing a publication, stop and ask "Why?". Why are you producing it? Is it necessary? Who is it for? How will you use it? What is its purpose? Is it being written to inform? To educate? To raise money? By answering these questions, you will have a clear idea of what you are producing before you even put pen to paper. You will also avoid falling into the trap of producing unnecessary material.

People with different needs

At an early stage you should also consider whether your publications, or some of them at least, need to be produced in minority languages. If this is a route you want to go down, use your local community relations council to advise you on the main languages spoken in your area, and to put you in touch with translators. Remember that typesetting in some languages is something that not all printers can handle. It can be costly, in terms of time as well as money, to get material typeset and printed in minority languages, particularly those which use a different script (such as Hindi, Chinese or Greek). Build this cost into your budget and your timetable. Proofreading also has to be budgeted for – I once came across a charity which had inserted a couple of paragraphs in Hindi into one of its leaflets, but not being Hindi-speakers, the staff had not realised that the Hindi text was upside down!

Producing material in other languages will inevitably raise expectations with the readers. If you produce a leaflet in Bengali, you'll need to ensure that you are geared up to take calls from Bengali speakers, or to reply to their letters in the right language, so think it all through carefully first.

Publications in large print (for people with visual impairments) or in Braille might also be worth considering. Perhaps some of your users would welcome your material on cassette tape, because they are blind, illiterate or their first language is not English. There are 1.7 million people in the UK with a visual disability, yet the majority of these people can read print if it is of a sufficient size and uses a clear typeface. The Royal National Institute for the Blind recommends a minimum point size of 14 for material aimed at partially sighted people. Their other recommendations are:

- use unjustified right margins (the text is aligned with the margin on the left, but ragged on the right hand margin)
- opt for matt paper – print on glossy paper can be hard to read, as can thin, semi-transparent paper
- leave spaces between paragraphs
- go for minimal use of capital letters – some partially sighted people can recognise the shape of words, but words in upper case lose their distinctive shape
- aim for short line lengths – no more than 65 characters
- achieve good contrast: ideally black type on white or yellow paper – but never yellow ink on white paper, which is practically invisible to partially sighted people
- use dark inks if black cannot be used, but never on dark paper avoid type running across photos or illustrations – it looks great from the design point of view but is difficult to read for many people
- use even word spacing.

For most charities, money is tight, and many desirables (such as using a design consultancy or opting for full colour printing) may be beyond reach. Nevertheless, it is important that you produce good publications, albeit on a shoestring budget. The following tips will help you to produce better publications for no extra outlay.

A BAKER'S DOZEN: BETTER PUBLICATIONS FOR NO EXTRA DOUGH!

1. **Don't battle against the clock.** Allow enough time to do the job well. Creating the necessary time and staff resources to allow a comfortable schedule will produce a better result, so plan well and start in plenty of time. Rush and you might end up paying more for your suppliers, you'll not have sufficient time to write the copy

well or to check it for errors, and you'll end up with a poorer publication that looks as if it was produced in a hurry.

2. **Keep quiet about your leeway.** Prepare a production schedule, copy it to your designer, printer, and to staff involved in the process, but allow plenty of leeway in it for inevitable slippages. Don't tell anyone about the leeway – it's your own insurance policy! Always meet the deadlines you have set yourself, as it saves a mad rush at the end to make up for lost time.

> **TRUE STORY**
>
> The following quote is from a letter I received from my solicitor about my new office: "For the avoidance of doubt, the subjects comprise the subjects with several rights and under the several obligations more particularly described in the draft disposition annexed and executed as relative hereto." If anyone knows what this means, perhaps they could get in touch. The Plain English campaign (see below) stress that even legal documents can be gobbledygook-free.

3. **Don't let your printer take you to the cleaners** – preparing a print specification could help save you money, by allowing you to compare like with like when you get print quotes. Get between three and five quotes, as prices vary enormously. You will probably have to pay more for rush jobs, so try to get it booked in with the printer.

4. **Steal!** They say that imitation is the sincerest form of flattery, so flatter a few charities by copying their good ideas, but adapting them to your own requirements. Get on as many charity mailing lists as you can, get hold of their reports and study them for good ideas. Do the same with company annual reports, and with magazines and brochures. If you see anything you like, copy it!

5. **Don't bother with bad photos**. Blurred photos, backs of heads, cheque presentations, figures in the distance or sitting around a table, people shaking hands – these are boring photos that you are better off without. If you don't have good quality pictures, find other ways of making your publication attractive. Consider buying a copyright-free book or disk if you can't afford a designer or photographer.

6. **Improve your circulation**. Circulate draft copy and allow time for staff to read and comment on it. Write deadlines on the copy and make it clear that comments received after that date cannot be incorporated. Give everyone guidelines on what sort of comments and amendments you want. If you don't, you will find that people start changing your wording when this is quite inappropriate, rather than just checking your copy for errors and omissions.

7. **Cut the waffle and get to the point**. Stick to the key facts, and be brutal about cutting anything that is not relevant.

TIP

Use caption photographs which are not self-explanatory. Your captions should add to the photo rather than just state the obvious. (Research has shown that more than anything else in reports and publications, it is the captions that are read, so don't miss out on this opportunity of getting your message across.)

8.   Use bite size chunks. Break up the text by using charts, graphics, bullet points, headlines, subheadings, box stories, different typefaces and type sizes (in moderation) and other devices, where appropriate. This will make your document or leaflet easier to read and more attractive. If you are using a designer, clever use of 'reversed out' text (see glossary) will give the illusion of an extra colour.

9.   Get personal. Use personal stories to help bring your publication to life. Charities come across so many appealing or moving stories, and yet few use them in their publications, perhaps for fear of exploitation. You can change names and details, and still produce moving accounts that will convey emotion and life. It's not exploitation, it's using your assets to get the money or attention that will enable you to continue your work.

10.   Don't back off when it comes to the back page. So many publications have a blank back page. This can work if it is used as part of the overall design, but often it is simply a wasted opportunity.

11.   Wear a snazzy jacket. Your cover design can make or break a publication. However interesting your document, if the cover is dull, it is less likely to be picked up, more likely to be tossed, unread, into the nearest bin. Publishers invest in good book jacket design because that's often what sells the book. Remember that it's as cheap to print a good cover as a bad one.

12.   Write for the reader. The language you use should be appropriate for the audience. So should the content and the design.

13.   Be listless! So many annual reports and other documents have endless and boring lists of names. Drop them, or at least tuck them away at the back. If you must say thank you to lists of people, find another way if you can. Write a thank you letter, for example.

As well as ensuring that you do certain things, you should remember that there are things you should avoid........

THE SEVEN DEADLY SINS

1.   **Planning by committee.** Never do it unless you are intent on a nervous breakdown! Involve other people by all means, but make sure than someone has overall responsibility and that one person has the final say.

2.   **Using small print or unbroken copy** (pages of text with no subheadings, bullet points, illustrations or other devices to break

up blocks of text). It makes your publication appear uninviting and difficult to read. If your publications are not read, their production will be a waste of money and effort. Many people cannot see small print, so never go below 9 point, and aim for 10 or 11.

3. **Using cheap and glossy paper, or garish colours**. Many people think it looks nice. Designers, the experts, will tell you that it is tacky. A matt paper looks more attractive, so avoid the cheapo paper, but be careful not to appear too lavish. If you care about the Earth, consider using recycled or unbleached paper, the quality of which has improved enormously in recent years. It's also less expensive than it used to be, though it may still cost you a little more.

4. **Allowing boring or badly-written copy to get past you**. It rarely gets read and is a waste of everyone's time. People only read boring things if they have to, so always aim for clear, interesting and readable copy that is crying out to be read. (See the next chapter for some copywriting tips.)

5. **Assuming too much**. Never assume that things will get done just because people say so. Always check and chase people up. Don't assume people know what you mean. Be explicit.

6. **Being unprofessional when selecting suppliers** – designer, printer, copywriter. Take your time and take care. Get references, see samples of their work, haggle over the price, and always get quotes from several before making a decision. Specify everything fully and in writing. If you don't, you will definitely come unstuck, perhaps not this time or next, but it will happen. (See next chapter.)

7. **Letting egos get in the way!** You are not producing something to impress your committee or director, to display flattering photographs of them, or to carry their personal views, so keep control of their egos – and your own.

> **TIP**
>
> *Prepare a clear structure for your publication if it is long (such as an annual report). For example, the structure might say that there will be a half page introduction, one-page cameos on the work of each of your ten different sections, two case histories, one photograph on each page, and a concluding statement by your director. Get it agreed by all involved, as this will save time-consuming and confusing changes or disagreements at a later stage. It will also make the copywriting task easier.*

Now for a look at the three main publications you are likely to produce:
- annual reports
- leaflets
- newsletters

ANNUAL REPORTS

By its very nature the annual report has a long shelf-life. Something that's going to last you for a whole year, and that will probably be your showpiece, deserves special treatment. The first thing about annual reports is that they take time, and usually more than you realise. If you start work on your report three months before your AGM you've missed the boat. Allow at least six months from initial planning to delivery if you want a comfortable schedule and a better end product.

Getting started is always the hardest bit. Get your previous reports and list what works well about each of them, as well as identifying the aspects of copy, design and format that are less successful. Translate these into a checklist of do's and don'ts. Do the same with other people's annual reports, making a careful note of anything that works particularly well. Include colleagues in this process if you can, for it helps to get other ideas and perspectives and it makes them feel involved.

The next step is to plan and structure the content. The mistake of most reports is that they follow a very rigid and traditional structure guaranteed to switch off all but the very dedicated reader. This usually involves an opening statement by the chairperson, followed by a page about each department or section of the organisation, and concluding with a page or so of financial information, more often than not presented in a boring way using badly produced bar charts and pie charts. If this sounds like your report, read on!

Rather than follow a department by department format for your report, which can be dull, consider doing a themed report. Think of an appropriate theme and write your report around it. You'll find that it's much more accessible and it is naturally held together by the theme.

The usual approach with an annual report is to ask the relevant members of staff to write their own contribution on their section's work, and the various manuscripts are then bundled together and sent off to the designer or printer. Not surprisingly, they read as if they have been written by half a dozen different people. You can avoid this by getting an editor (either a professional one, or a literate member of staff) to connect the contributions to each other, integrate them around your chosen theme, delete any repetitions, and unify the style. The end result will be a great deal more readable.

Most organisations aim to put everything into their annual report rather than just the highlights or the bits that fit the theme. It's far better to give a readable flavour of your work than to pack the pages with the full detail, most of which will be ignored by most of your readers.

These days companies are producing much less formal reports and you can take a tip from them. Many now look more like magazines than staid reports. Design is playing an increasing role, particularly when it comes to the presentation of financial information. Old-style bar and pie charts have been given the boot, in favour of more imaginative graphic representations of information.

When it comes to your financial facts, do remember that you do not necessarily have to include your full accounts as part of your annual report; they can be produced as a separate insert, and many charities are opting to do this, sending the insert only to those who are actually interested in the financial nitty gritty. The annual report then generally includes just a brief outline of the financial position, with a sentence to say that the full accounts are available on request.

And finally to the vexed question of lists. Pick up a dozen charity annual reports and see how many of them feature list upon list. There will be the list of staff, the list of committee members, the list of advisers such as the bank, solicitors etc. With any list, start by asking if it is needed. If it is, at least make it interesting. For example, when listing your committee don't just state A.J. Baron, B. Smith, P. Singh etc. Say something a bit more meaningful which gives an insight into why they are on your committee, for example: Anthea Baron – Anthea has served on our committee for three years, allowing us to benefit from her ten years' experience as Chair of Recreation and Director of Play Parks for Kids.

> **TRUE STORY**
> I once received a beautifully produced charity annual report. It looked really good but there was something not quite right about it. Then I spotted what it was: the year covered by the report was missing from the cover! It's easily done so be careful not to make that mistake yourself.

LEAFLETS

I have yet to come across a charity or voluntary organisation that does not have at least one leaflet. When producing a leaflet, you need to be clear about its purpose so that the words and design are appropriate. Generally, a leaflet falls into one of the following four categories:
- information leaflets
- promotional leaflets
- campaigning leaflets
- publicity leaflets

> **TIP**
> *Be imaginative with titles for publications. Don't just call your annual report "Annual Report", for example. Think of something a bit catchier, such as "Child's Play: Anytown Toy Library's Annual Report for 1999".*

Information leaflets

Leaflets created to inform (such as a welfare rights leaflet) are often the easiest to write. The 'questions and answers' format works best here, where you ask the questions that the reader will want addressed, then go on to answer them. It's as simple as that. A question is also a good device for the front cover e.g. Want to know more about your rights?

Promotional leaflets

A leaflet to promote your organisation can be a difficult one to put together, for it can be hard to cover everything you do without getting too wordy. A good strategy is simply to go for the 'feel good factor'. In other words try to present a flavour of what you do rather than go into the detail, with the aim of leaving the reader feeling that you are a worthwhile cause or organisation. They don't need to understand everything that you do in order to feel good about you.

Campaigning leaflets

A mistake made by many campaigns is that they produce an informative leaflet about the campaign, but the leaflet fails to tell the reader what they can do to help or support. All campaigning leaflets need to contain:

- information about the campaign, including powerful facts and figures
- a short case study, if appropriate, to provide human interest
- a list of things people can do to help or support
- a contact for further information/membership details

TIP

Be imaginative with titles for publications. Don't just call your annual report "Annual Report," for example. Think of something a bit catchier, such as "Child's Play: Anytown Toy Library's Annual Report for 1995".

There's no point in persuading people that you are worth supporting if you don't explain how they can become involved. Once you've interested them enough to get potential supporters to read your leaflet, it's always best to get them to sign up there and then, by returning a membership application slip. That's far better than leaving it up to the reader to make contact by phone or letter to request further information. They may not bother, or by the time it arrives their enthusiasm may have worn off.

Publicity leaflets

These are leaflets designed to promote something – a conference or training course perhaps. You should aim to make such leaflets as easy to reply to as possible. The tear-off slip is a good device here, but if you are using one make sure that you:

a) include the return address on the tear-off bit

b) don't put any essential information on the back of the tear-off part

The majority of leaflets are A4 folded to either A5 (half A4) or to a third A4. Which to go for depends on three factors:

1) how you intend to distribute them. If by post, which size will fit most easily into your standard envelopes?
2) for leaflets which are to be displayed, will they be put into leaflet holders? If so, what size are they?
3) some copy naturally fits a leaflet that is folded twice. Some fits better on an A5 leaflet. Take advice from your designer if you are using one.

NEWSLETTERS

Whether it's for staff, supporters or service-users, your newsletter should be a readable and well written document. Here are ten tips to think about:

NATTY NEWSLETTERS:
Ten tips that won't cost a penny

1. Use good headlines. If you don't know what works well, take a look at newspapers, which are expert in the art of headline writing. A memorable one about a fighter pilot returning to the war zone read: PILOT FLIES BACK TO FRONT.

2. Always use a strong cover photo.

3. Try to have regular features so that readers know what to expect and become familiar with the newsletter. They're more likely to develop an attachment to it that way.

4. Aim for a mix of longer articles and plenty of snippets.

5. Number your newsletter and add the month or season of publication. That way readers know if they have missed an issue.

6. Do a trailer for one or two items that you will feature in the next issue.

7. Only include material that will appeal to the majority of your readers.

8. If you don't have a letters page, consider introducing one. It turns your newsletter from a one-way communication to a two-way one.

9. Publish the copy deadline for the next issue if you want to encourage contributions.

10. Remember that most articles will benefit from editing, so get the red pen out!

Another way of making your newsletter better is to find out what your readers think about it. Every year or two you should do a readership questionnaire to discover which features are popular, which are not, whether readers like the style of writing, the design, the photos etc. As an incentive to encourage readers to reply, consider a prize draw (though remember that that will mean that feedback cannot be anonymous).

> **TIP**
> *Never ask a question in a headline unless readers will answer it with a 'yes'.*

If you have a newsletter that comes out frequently, it can be tricky finding enough information to fill it. Here's some inspiration:

Ten ideas for regular newsletter features

1. Book reviews
2. A quiz
3. Hellos .... welcome to new staff or members
4. Goodbyes .... farewell to staff retiring or leaving
5. Spotlight – a profile of a supporter or member of staff
6. Focus – a closer look at the work of a relevant or related organisation
7. Profile – a look at one of your departments or offices
8. Fact file/Did you know? – a different fact every month e.g. "We receive 100,000 enquiries each year" or "Did you know that the office uses 9,000 gallons of water each month?"
9. A letters page
10. Soap box/What gets my goat – a chance for readers to sound off about any issue

Ten ides for one-off features

1. When I grow up – ask a selection of staff or members what they wanted to be when they were little
2. Crystal ball – ask relevant people where they believe your organisation will be in 100 years time
3. Bouncing babies – get photos of staff when they were babies and run a competition to match the name to the baby
4. For your January issue do a piece on people's new year's resolutions. Follow up the following year to see if they kept them!
5. Pictures of the past – publish photos from years back, of your work, premises or staff
6. Pages from the past – reproduce some front covers from newsletters you published years ago
7. Do a special themed issue – e.g. a 'green' issue with tips on recycling, saving the planet, articles on the environment etc. Print it in green ink on recycled paper.
8. What the papers say – run an occasional round-up of press coverage you have received
9. Do a special anniversary issue for a landmark year – look back at the issues of the day
10. Logo low-down – explain how you got your logo and what it symbolises. Feature other organisations' logos too.

GET YOUR PUBLICATIONS TO EARN THEIR KEEP

Remember to make your publications work for you. Don't spend money on leaflets and then leave them sitting in a box in a storeroom. Ensure that your staff, volunteers and committee know what publications you produce and that they receive a copy of everything new, with a covering letter explaining its purpose and audience. Urge staff to take copies of publications to hand out at conferences, meetings and seminars. Have supplies at reception and in other places where they can be seen by your target audiences, such as GPs' surgeries, community centres and libraries. Send leaflets and other publications out to enquirers and with other mailings as appropriate. And don't forget that some of your publications will contain newsworthy information, so send copies to your local media with a news release attached.

Increasingly, charities are producing publications for sale. The bigger charities and campaign groups have been doing this for many years, but if you are just starting out in the sales game, it's important that you get your marketing right or you could end up out of pocket.

You will need to find ways of letting people know what you publish (by, for example, sending out review copies to target publications, with the aim of some free coverage; by advertising, if appropriate; and by mailing your publications lists to possible purchasers – bookshops, organisations and individuals).

You should consider promotions and special offers, such as 'Buy one and get a second at half price' or 'Spend over £20 and get your postage and packing free.'

You will also need to make it as easy as possible for buyers to order from you, by producing simple order forms and an uncomplicated but fair formula for charging for postage, package and insurance. Never get into publishing for profit unless you have carried out careful market research, and devised a realistic business plan and marketing strategy.

> **TIP**
>
> *Newspapers produce a 'house style' guide to ensure consistency. With so many journalists writing for them, it is necessary to set down guidelines on how things should be done. You might find it useful to prepare one if you produce a lot of publications or have many people contributing to them. Here are some examples of what you might include:*
>
> - *always spell out numbers from one to ten*
> - *use numerals for 11 onwards*
> - *use full names at the first mention, but thereafter the first name only*
> - *commonly known abbreviations such as BBC or IBM are fine, but spell out at first mention ones likely to be unfamiliar to the reader.*

CHAPTER SIX

COPYWRITING

It is pointless spending money on great photography, stylish design and quality printing if your publications never get read. Sure, design can help make a document easier to read, but good design is no substitute for good copy. The whole point about writing is that it is produced to be read. Yet no one will bother unless the writing is worth reading. This chapter will help improve your writing ability, boost your confidence when it comes to writing, and pass on some top copywriting tips.

Public relations is about communication: publications are merely communication tools. You may be relieved to hear that to communicate effectively in writing, you don't have to be a top-selling author, you don't have to be a successful journalist, and you don't have to be an expert in grammar. Yes, it's true! It is quite normal (even for professional copywriters) to feel anxious about writing. Will the copy be readable? Will it be up to scratch? Will you make silly grammatical errors? If you worry about your writing ability, relax! There are some basic rules that can be easily and quickly grasped, turning you overnight into a better wordsmith.

BANISHING GOBBLEDEGOOK

The first rule of copywriting is dead easy: always use plain English – whatever audience you are writing for. Most organisations have their own jargon: be careful to avoid it, particularly in anything you are producing for service-users and the general public. If you are not sure whether what you have written is comprehensible to a layperson, get a friend who does not work in your field to read through it.

If there is no alternative to your jargon, be sure to explain what it means. Also make sure that you don't use any unexplained acronyms.

Avoiding jargon is important, but that's just one aspect of writing interesting and readable copy.

TRUE STORY

Big companies have been quick to see commercial advantage in operating a plain English policy, but the voluntary sector has (surprisingly) been much slower to see the benefits. Here's an extract from a leaflet I received from British Telecom, showing how far things have improved in the commercial sector: "As you'll see if you look through the rest of this booklet, we've also made our Conditions a little easier to digest. For a start, we've cut out the jargon. We've spelled out all your rights under BT's Customer Service Guarantee, and we've sub-divided the information into logical sections ..."

I like their down-to-earth and friendly style. Do your publications use this easy and accessible style?

TIP

If you would like to know more about producing clear copy and well-designed, easy-to-complete forms, there are two organisations you should contact for advice.

The Plain English Campaign is a self-funding, non-profit organisation founded in 1979 to promote the advantages of clear communication. It produces an 'A - Z Guide of Alternative Words' and a pack on how to write letters in plain English. Investing in one could help you improve your image!

The Plain English Campaign, PO Box 3, New Mills, Stockport SK12 4QP. Tel. 01663 734541

Also get in touch with the Plain Language Commission, set up by the co-founder of the Plain English Campaign. For a fee they will edit text for adverts, mailings and any other material. They can also help ensure your design aids clarity. Both these organisations offer training and a plain English 'kitemark'. The Plain Language Commission, The Castle, 29 Stoneheads, Whaley Bridge, Stockport SK12 7BB. Tel. 01663 733177.

To produce clear, crisp copy in-house, made sure you address the following before you put pen to paper:

1) the **FUNCTION** of the publication: do you want a flyer that can be quickly and easily read? A poster with a clear message that needs to be read at some distance? How will your publication be used?

2) the **READER**: who are you writing for? professionals? the public? an informed audience? people with learning disabilities?

3) the **CONTENT**: what are the main points you wish to convey: clarify your thoughts before you begin to write, and jot down your key points.

When you write something, you cannot use the other ways of communicating that come into play when we speak, such as stress, intonation and body language. It is therefore vital that you choose your words carefully so that they convey the right message. Know what you want to say and say it as clearly as you can.

TRUE STORY

I was asked to give a lecture to a university department specialising in print production, communication and publishing. When I called the number printed on their letterhead to confirm arrangements, the number was unobtainable. It turned out that the department had misprinted its number on 10,000 letterheads. Make sure your material is accurate in every detail.

WRITE ON: THE ABC OF GOOD WRITING

Always apply the ABC of good writing:

Accuracy – check spellings, phone numbers, facts...

Brevity – say what you need to say and no more

Clarity – check that your meaning is clear and unambiguous.

Follow these tips for copywriting made easy and you will begin to find that it becomes just that – easy.

COPYWRITING MADE EASY

- Ask yourself with every sentence you write, 'What am I really trying to say?'

- Have a mental picture of your reader. If possible, write for a real person rather than a type, such as an ABC1 male.

- Talk to your reader as if you were sitting in the same room. Apply the test: 'If I were saying this face to face, would I use these words?'

- Use the 'first person' – 'I', 'you' – to make documents so much more personal and easier to identify with.

- Be natural when you write. You don't have to adopt a formal style, nor should you sound pompous or stuffy. Some people use long or unusual words to show off; they fail to see that a well-written document is a readable document, and that's what impresses.

- Vary the length of your sentences, with a mix of short, medium and longer ones, but try not to use too many sentences (like this one) which contain more than 25 words, as they can start to get a little difficult to follow!

- Make your writing more accessible and informal by using contractions – I'll, you're, don't etc.

- Use short words, sentences and paragraphs. Try to create readable 'chunks.'

- Avoid jargon. It can be a useful device if both writer and reader understand the language – it's alienating if they don't.

- Check every sentence to make sure that the reader can understand it without having to read it twice. If you find this difficult, get someone else to look over it for you.

- And finally, ignore unnecessary grammatical rules and forget what you were told at school – it's OK to start a sentence with 'And' or 'But', as has just been demonstrated!

BREAK UP THE TEXT

It's not how long your material is, but how long the reader thinks is it that counts. Dense, unbroken text will look longer than it actually is. So find ways to break up the text and signpost your reader to the key bits of text. Try using:

- boxed-off text
- pull-quotes
- bulletpoints
- subheadings

A common mistake when writing is to be too inward-looking. What excites you and your organisation may not interest the outside world. Focus on your readers' needs and interests. Always write from their perspective, not on your own. Rambling opening statements from your chairperson are a bore. They might make your committee happy, but will turn your reader off. Remember that your aim is riveted readers who keep on reading.

COPYWRITING TECHNIQUES

There is no simple formula you can follow for guaranteed writing success. But there are tips and techniques that can help ease the writing task and improve the end result. Here are some of the most common, most effective, and most easy to apply copywriting techniques. See how you can use them to spice up your writing style.

Alliteration

Alliteration is the use of similar sounds at the beginning of neighbouring words. Here's a rather contrived fictitious example to illustrate the point: 'Coasters convalescent cottages provide quality care and compassion to help you continue to cope'. I have used the technique myself above, where I suggest that you should aim for riveted readers who keep on reading.

Puns

The pun (a play on words) can be very effective, especially for slogans and staplines. For example, a service counselling people addicted to gambling might ask: 'Can we help? You bet we can!'. However, beware the unintentional pun. I came across the following on the menu of a family-friendly Indian restaurant: 'Let your children watch as we bake their nan in front of them.' (Where I come from a 'nan' is a grandmother, not unleavened bread!)

Rhyme

Rhyme is another time-tested copywriting device that has proved its value. When the government launched a clampdown on benefits fraud it asked: 'Know of a benefit rip-off? Give us a telephone tip-off. Call the Beat-A-Cheat Line.'

Antonyms

An antonym is a word that means the opposite (as opposed to a synonym, which is a word that has the same meaning). How about this one for a knicker manufacturer: 'The big name in smalls' (yes, I made that one up!) or this equally unlikely example which illustrates the point: 'We're the tops for bottoms' (fictitious advert for a nappy cream).

You can use this technique with words that are not, strictly speaking, antonyms. Here's a real-life example, the slogan from an advert for hair-removing cream: Takes minutes, lasts weeks.

Unexpected deviance

No it's not an arrestable offence! Take a list or a series of sentences, each following a pattern. Ensure that the last one in the list deviates unexpectedly from that pattern. Here's an example from Virgin Direct Personal Financial Service: 'Good quality, good value, good service and good riddance to salesmen!'.

REVISE, REVISE, REVISE

Few people can turn out great copy straight off. Most of us plan our writing, draft and then redraft (often many times) until we come up with a version that is acceptable to us – or until we run out of time! Don't expect to be able to write wonderful material first time round. Build-in time to revise and improve your work.

When it comes to revising your writing, look out for the following:

- stilted text – if it jars, rewrite
- inappropriate words or sections – take them out
- over-use of the same words or phrases – consult a thesaurus for alternatives
- repetition of information – edit
- clichés – find fresher ways to express yourself
- irrelevancies – edit
- redundant words e.g. join together, meet up with (redundancies in italics) – edit
- ambiguity and lack of clarity – rewrite so the meaning is crystal clear
- consistency – for example, if you hyphenate the word 'co-ordinate' in the first paragraph, do so throughout
- dense, unbroken text – employ the techniques described above to create readable chunks
- omissions – make sure all the vitals are included
- jargon – translate into plain English
- aptness of language – check that the choice of words is appropriate for the audience
- variety in sentence length – check for a mix of short, medium and long.

> **TIP**
>
> *When you write some copy, put it away for a few days and try to forget about it. Return to it refreshed and you are more likely to see its shortcomings.*

> **TIP**
>
> *Sometimes revision is not enough. If you are really unhappy with what you have written, it is often better (and quicker in the long run) to start again from scratch. Never feel that chucking your work in the bin is a waste. It may be a necessary step on the journey to a piece of punchy, lively or persuasive copy.*

HAVE A GO YOURSELF

So now you know what to look out for and what to do to add a bit of sparkle to your writing style. Time to put it to the test. Try your editing and copywriting skills on the following passage from a fictitious annual report. Cut out anything unnecessary and do what you can to make it less boring, less introspective, more lively and more readable. Be as brutal as you like and remember that good editors have razor-sharp pencils.

THE DUMBLETOWN MEN'S HOSTEL: ANNUAL REPORT
INTRODUCTION

As Acting Chairman of the Dumbletown Men's Hostel I would like to offer my sincere and heartfelt thanks to the committee, who have given their time and effort all year to enable the hostel to run smoothly. In particular I would like to single out Dorothy Grainger, my able Vice Chairman, who has been a marvel. Thanks must also go to the very committed staff for their loyal service – everyone from the Hostel Manager at the top, through to the team of devoted cleaners who have carried out a very necessary job. And while on the subject of 'thank yous', I should like to thank the various Dumbletown businesses who have most generously donated to the cause during the year, especially the Dumbletown Furniture Company, Fred Windsor's Carpet Factory, the Davies and Jones Partnership and, of course, our excellent bankers MidWest and our solicitors Whinney, Chelford and Glinney.

The last year has been a busy one, with more men using the facility than ever before. We also held a record number of committee meetings, with one session lasting until nearly midnight! We have added a new wing to the hostel, which now enables us to cater for an extra ten men each night. Previously we could house a total of 20 men, so the new wing has increased our capacity by 50%, which means that we are now able to make a much larger contribution to helping homeless men in the town.

Finding move-on accommodation is a priority for us, with many of our clients requiring supported accommodation after dispensing with the services of our facility. For such clients, we liaise with our partners in the local authority social work department, with staff at the health authority and in the housing department, and with local housing providers such as housing associations and housing co-operatives in the area, to ensure that their move-on needs are met. Thanks to excellent relationships with the statutory authorities, and with the local voluntary sector, we are finding move-on and supported accommodation at a much faster rate, and we are securing permanent accommodation for many of our cases.

Next year we will seek to ensure that our hostel continues to give the high standard of service that our clients have come to expect from the hostel facility. So once again, many thanks to all those who have been involved in making the project such a great success during the last 12 months.

The example above, while fictitious and perhaps a little exaggerated, is not so different from real life annual report opening statements to be found, sadly, in far too many charity annual reports. What was wrong with it?

- The most striking feature is that apart from a few sentences it's one big 'thank you'.

- Clearly it has been written not for an external audience, but for, in this order, committee members (particularly Dorothy Grainger), staff (particularly the Manager), and local businesses which have donated money. There is nothing wrong with thanking these people, but a personal letter would be more appropriate. It's amazing how many charities feel they should use their annual report to thank suppliers such as banks, auditors and solicitors. You are paying them for the service, so they should be thanking you!

- It is too inward-looking, and references to the number and length of meetings is of no interest to the average reader. What's more important – the meetings or the men?

- Talking about the hostel as a 'facility' and the men as 'clients' and worse, as 'cases' is cold, impersonal and inappropriate.

- The language used conveys a lot about the values of the organisation. The use of 'Chairman' makes it sound out-of-touch and sexist.

- Its emphasis on hierarchy and its patronising reference to cleaners also conveys a sense that the organisation is old-fashioned.

- The use of jargon such as 'move-on', 'supported accommodation' and 'hostel facility' is unhelpful.

- The conclusion sounds a bit complacent – as if the hostel is not striving to be better, but only to stand still.

- The headlines/titles are unimaginative.

Now that you've had a go at rewriting the passage above, compare what you have done with the version on the following page.

GIVING DUMBLETOWN MEN A ROOF: THE ANNUAL REPORT OF THE DUMBLETOWN MEN'S HOSTEL

MORE MEN HOUSED THANKS TO NEW WING

Thanks to our new wing, more men in Dumbletown had a roof over their head last year, and many more have been found homes of their own.

Working in partnership with the council and health authority, we have been able to ensure than men leaving the hostel get the help and support they need to find their feet again, and to get established in their new homes.

The emphasis has been on partnerships this year, with our most notable successes being due to everyone working together to find solutions. Local businesses worked with us to help fund the new wing, our staff worked in teams to support the men using the hostel, and our committee pulled together to ensure that the project expanded, enabling us to house an extra ten men every night.

We intend to spend the next year building upon the achievements of this one. A top priority is to ensure that we continue to provide homeless men with the care, support and service that they deserve – and that we work hard to expand our service, and to provide higher quality care, in better surroundings. We can do this only if we nurture and strengthen the partnerships which have proved so successful this year.

DISCUSSION

This is a great deal better, but what makes it so?

- It has a theme – partnerships – which runs through it
- It is less inward-looking, focusing on the users of the hostel, rather than the committee and staff
- It is shorter and more readable
- It contains no jargon
- It contains no unnecessary detail
- It does not have boring 'thank yous', although it does recognise and acknowledge the role of others in the success of the hostel
- The headlines/titles are snappier

CHAPTER SEVEN

USING DESIGNERS AND PRINTERS

Most charities have to deal with printers at some time, and many also use designers. Getting the best out of them involves understanding how they work and what they need from you. This chapter will give you an insight into designers' and printers' needs, introduce you to some of their jargon, and give you a chance to pick up some useful tips. It also deals with logos and corporate identity.

There's no doubt that being a designer is a trendy occupation. Tell someone at a party that you are a teacher or an accountant and their eyes will glaze over, but say you're a designer and prepare for an altogether more positive reaction. We think of designers as fashionable young things in flash specs with striking ties/earrings, gliding creatively around the drawing boards in their tastefully decorated design studio. This frightens us. We feel worried about approaching them for fear that our ideas will be ridiculed, considered too boring, or that we will be unable to afford the bill. Relax. Once you understand how to use a designer and how to get the best out of one, you will have overcome your fear.

DESIGNS ON YOU!

There are many talented freelance designers, so using a designer does not have to mean using an expensive design company. Sadly, though, finding a good designer is not like finding a milkman. Not all designers are the same, even if they have received identical training from the same college. Some have limited creativity and a very set style of work, others are capable of great variation and have tackled wide-ranging assignments. A good way to find a designer is by recommendation, so if you have never used one before, ask friends and colleagues if they can give you some names. Look through other charity annual reports, and if any stand out, get in touch and ask them who did the design work. If all this fails, Yellow Pages always provide a last resort, although you are only likely to find design consultancies advertising there; freelance designers will probably not be listed.

Visit several designers and see their work. Also check for reliability: your chosen designer might be very talented, but if they are unreliable, you could be in for problems, so do get references if you are unsure – talk to their clients and ask whether they are good at meeting deadlines. The same goes for your other suppliers.

Once you select a designer, you will need to explain what your organisation does, what sort of publications it produces (give copies to your designer), and what you are expecting from the assignment.

Briefing Designers

Even a great designer will not produce a good job for you if they are given a lousy brief. Spending time talking to your designer will pay off in the end. For any design job you will need to supply some of the following information. How much you specify depends on how many decisions you are happy to allow your designer to make. If you are unsure, defer to the designer.

- **COLOURS:** How many colours do you want to use? (The more colours, the higher the cost for design and print.) What colours? What about halftones (see page 111)?

- **COPY:** How much copy (text) will there be? (How many words?) Which bits of copy need to be placed where? If you have already written the copy, let the designer see it.

- **SIZE:** How many pages do you want your finished document to be? (An A4 document is produced by folding A3 sheets, so remember that pages go up in multiples of four, i.e. if you planned on a 12-page document, but you now need to lengthen it, you must opt for 16 pages.) What size of page?

- **FOLDING:** Will your leaflet be folded? If so, what type of fold? (There are many different ways of folding paper and some, such as staggered concertinas, to use a technical term, are more expensive to carry out and more complicated to design to than traditional folds such as gatefolds. Your designer will show you different types of folds and explain the pros and cons.)

- **VISUALS:** How many visuals do you plan to use? Where do you want them placed? What type of visuals (photos; illustrations; charts; tables; cartoons)? Who will provide them – you or the designer? (Using a picture library will cost you money, so if you have good photographs, use them.) The more charts and illustrations you ask your designer to originate, the bigger the bill you will receive for the work – illustration is much more time-consuming than straightforward page layout.

- **GUIDELINES:** How much freedom does the designer have? Even if it's a lot, also give a few guidelines or some sort of briefing. Be clear on where the designer can make decisions, and where you want to have a say.

■ **'LOOK':** What is the style or 'look' of your publication? Do you want something expensive-looking, with quality paper and classy illustrations, or a more modest affair on thinner paper and with fewer colours and pictures?

■ **FUNCTION:** What is the function of the publication you are producing? A poster that needs to be seen at a distance? An information pack that will be read cover to cover?

■ **AUDIENCE:** Who will read your publication? People with learning difficulties? Children? Professionals? Young people? The intended audience will influence the design.

■ **PAPER:** You will need to decide on the type of paper you want. Paper manufacturers give names to their paper, just as car makers brand their vehicles. Do you want a textured paper, a recycled one, something that is transparent or has a special coating? There are so many types available. A decision will also need to be taken on the paper's weight (paper is described according to its weight in grammes per square metre or 'gsm'. Letterheads are normally around 100gsm and magazine covers are generally 220gsm to 250gsm.) The colour of paper must be selected from a large variety. Your designer should be able to advise you on all of these, show you samples, and give you a rough idea of price. Try to avoid glossy paper, as it looks tacky, does not take ink as well as matt paper, and looks grubby sooner, attracting fingerprints and creases.

■ **TYPE:** What typeface would you like? (Ask to see samples.) And what point size (size of type)? Do you want the type to be right hand justified or unjustified? (In other words, do you want the text to have a ragged edge on the right hand side, or to have a straight right hand margin, as with your left hand margin?) Do you want columns of text, as in newspapers? If so, how many? What 'weight' of type? Bold or normal, for example.

Your designer should offer you guidance on many of the above points, and indeed you are paying for their best advice on

> **TIP**
>
> *If you opt for a heavier paper for your publication, it may affect the postage you have to pay when you mail it, thus pushing up your overall costs in a way you have not budgeted for.*

> **FACT**
> Did you know that there are thousands of different typefaces or 'fonts'? Thanks to clever computer technology, typefaces can now be manipulated to create new fonts. Here are just a few, to show the wide variety:
>
> Times Roman and TIMES ROMAN
> Courier and COURIER
> Monaco and MONACO
> **Helvetica compressed** and **HELVETICA COMPRESSED**
> *Swing* and *SWING*
>
> Use an original typeface by all means (as long as it is easy on the eye) but don't mix too many fonts, or you will end up with a clutter. In addition to a great range of fonts, there are also many different point sizes (or sizes of typeface). The main text in this book is point size 10 (including this sentence).
>
> This is point size 20.
> # This is 30.

technical matter such as paper and typefaces, so they should be recommending materials and styles that will be appropriate for the job. If they are not good at advising, and you are unclear about your own ideas, don't use them. In any case, it's always worth talking to two or three designers to get different perspectives and different quotes for the work. However, having found a good and affordable designer, you might wish to stick with them, particularly if they begin to build up an understanding of your work and the image of your organisation.

Agree a fee and timescale before you proceed – and get it in writing. It will be your only comeback if things begin to slip.

DIY DESIGN

Don't worry if you can't afford a designer. While something professionally produced is going to be better, it is possible to produce acceptable material in-house. Many charities these days have desk top publishing (DTP) software on their computer, or access to equipment. However, a word of warning about DTP use in the hands of the keen novice: don't try to be over-ambitious if you are new to DTP. Going overboard with lots of different fonts and type sizes will make your publication look messy. Your computer might be capable of producing 40 different fonts, but you don't have to use them all! If at all possible, get some proper training before you start.

If you don't have access to DTP, it's possible to get a printer to do an imaginative typesetting and basic design job for you, although it will never be as good as something done by a professional designer.

CORPORATE IDENTITY

When it comes to corporate identity (see below for definition), it always helps to bring in the professionals for advice, though proceed with caution. Corporate identity is an area of work that lands many organisations, particularly charities and public sector ones, in trouble. The NHS hit the headlines in 1994 when it decided to revamp its identity and redesign its logo. £50,000 was spent on the process and the end result was little different. The media were in their element, criticising the NHS for wasting money. A consultant or several nurses could have been employed for the same money, according to the press. If you spend lots of money on design, your supporters and users might feel that you are mis-spending your funds or that you are more concerned with image than with important issues or service delivery. However, there are benefits in having a coherent corporate identity, and so long as you do not go overboard with an inappropriately flash image, you will hopefully have few critics and many admirers. A revamp of your identity can also serve as a media opportunity and a chance to freshen up your image and appeal more to your target audience.

But before we get into the pros and cons of a strong corporate identity, what exactly is corporate identity? It is about how your organisation presents itself visually to your publics. A logo is the main element of a corporate identity, but it's about so much more. Do you have corporate colours for your letterhead and publicity material? Are company vehicles (if you have them) in the corporate colours, complete with logo? Is your reception area or front door painted in your colours? Do staff wear name badges with your logo on, or uniforms (such as sweat shirts) in the appropriate colours? Is your logo used in job advertisements? Don't miss an opportunity to get your message across in this way and to reinforce your charity's visual identity.

Having a strong visual identity need not be monotonous, and it is undoubtedly a good way of reinforcing your presence and encouraging quick recognition among supporters and the public. The more they are exposed to it, the sooner they will come to associate your colours with your organisation, and to recognise your logo.

Try to be imaginative with the application of your identity, and to take advantage of every opportunity to get it across. If you run a café as part of your project, why not have tablecloths in your colours? If you have window boxes or hanging baskets outside your office, plant them in flowers which bloom in your colours. Applying your identity can be fun, so don't limit yourself to your letterhead!

Some larger organisations and charities, and many public bodies such as local authorities and universities, produce design guidelines on the implementation of their corporate image (see sample on page 104). Unless you are a big organisation, with many offices or departments all producing their own publicity, there is probably no need for you to worry about this.

DESIGN GUIDELINES FOR CHILD'S PLAY
THE CHARITY FOR KIDS' PLAY SCHEMES NATIONALLY

INTRODUCTION

This design guide illustrates the main elements of our new visual image and style. The aim of having a coherent design is not to create dull conformity, but to present a strong and instantly recognised image.

COLOUR

Our logo is printed in red and black on white paper. To ensure that you get the right shade of red, you should tell printers that the red we use is "PMS 032". (PMS stands for pantone matching system, an international system used by printers for ensuring colour match.)

Tempting though it is to introduce new colours, it is important that you stick to the official colours, so that all our material has a unified look. If you are printing in black only, you will find that the logo reproduces well in black and white.

TYPEFACE

We use a typeface called Marker Felt Thin. If you are reproducing in colour, the words "Child's Play" should always appear in red. Body text should appear in black in a typeface called Palatino. You can use bold, regular or italicised text as appropriate.

LOGO

Our logo is an extremely versatile image and it's tempting to be creative with it, changing it to make it more interesting. Please don't. The logo should always appear as it does in this guide. Please use it on all publicity you produce.

POSITION

The logo should appear on the top right hand side of the page, with our name centred beneath it.

BROMIDES

The bromides (master artwork) enclosed with this contain some words and images that you might find useful. We have provided a limited number of sizes, but these can be enlarged or reduced as required.

If you are getting material printed in colour, you will need to contact our designer, Jennifer Jones, who will let you have some 'colour separated' artwork, which is ready for printing.

FURTHER APPLICATIONS

Our logo should be used on all stationery and publicity materials and on our vehicles and staff uniforms.

HELP!

We have produced these guidelines to help you create more attractive publicity, for internal and external use. Please follow them.

If you need any help at all on the design front, contact Jennifer Jones, in the PR department. She can answer your questions and put you in touch with printers, but don't forget that non-stock stationery requests should be cleared with the director first.

THE GOOD DESIGN CHECKLIST

Like art, design is a matter of taste, though it is possible to apply some objective criteria as a check that the design work you have commissioned is appropriate:

- ■ it should appeal to the target audience

- ■ the text should be easy to read and to follow, guiding your reader through the document or leaflet

- ■ the illustrations (cartoons, photos and drawings) should be appropriate for the audience

- ■ it should enhance your image

- ■ your logo should appear on it

- ■ it should not appear too cramped or crowded

- ■ neither should it be too blank or sparse

- ■ it should be well executed and neat/tidy

- ■ it should be appropriate for the use to which it will be put

- ■ it should make imaginative use of the colours available (this is particularly important if you have just one or two colours)

If you have picked a competent designer and provided a good brief, your artwork should fit the bill. Sadly, though, not all artwork lives up to expectations, and it is helpful to be able to identify why the design doesn't work.

SPOTTING DESIGN FAULTS

You would think that spotting bad design would be easy, for it would look terrible. The trouble is that much bad design actually looks really good; what makes it poor is that it is either inappropriate for the audience or for the use to which it is to be put.

Never go for a design just because you like it; always choose a style that will appeal to the audience the material is aimed at. So a psychedelic leaflet with 3D cover may not be the best choice for a leaflet on welfare rights for pensioners! Equally, traditional design may not appeal to teenagers. So design that looks good is only part of the picture, it must be appropriate too.

Six common design faults

1. Text that is difficult to follow due to the way it has been laid out – it lacks a visual eyepath to direct the reader.

2. Material that is hard to read due to small print or clashing colours which make the text 'dance' before your eyes.

3. Material that is not very user-friendly because text has been superimposed on an illustration.

4. Material that fails to use typographical tricks to catch the readers' attention – such as callouts, boxes and bullet points.

5. A document that looks wrong for the purpose, such as a serious annual report that looks like a cheap newsletter, or a free brochure that looks so glossy that people are afraid to take one.

6. Design work that uses graphic devices to highlight words or phrases that are not the most important or interesting bits – your design should ensure that the best bits leap out from the page, so that if these alone are read, the reader will have picked up the key information.

TALKING TO DESIGNERS ABOUT LOGOS

The main element of a corporate identity is the logo, as its colours and design set the style for everything else. We said above that it can be acceptable to produce basic design work in-house, but when it comes to a logo, it is best that you invest in a designer, because logo design is far more complicated, yet far less costly, than many people realise. (Having said that, some big companies have been criticised for spending tens or even hundreds of thousands of pounds on a new logo, such as British Telecom when they introduced their stylish winged messenger logo in the early 1990s. It is possible, however, to get a new logo for not much more than £100, if you select and brief your designer carefully.)

But before you start talking to designers, talk to each other. Decide what sort of a logo you want, what image you want to portray through your logo, and whether the logo needs to incorporate any words. Will your logo be a design in its own right (such as Mothercare's or Shell's) or will it be a stylised version of your name (like Harrods' or Coca Cola's)? Will you have a strapline? (See below.) Take your time over this, and never rush into a new logo, as you will have to live with any mistakes for a very long time.

Once you have agreed among yourselves about what you are looking for (never an easy task when it comes to something as personal and subjective as a logo!), brief your designer. The designer will come up with rough drawings for several quite different logos for you to look at, react to and comment on, before presenting you with finished artwork. When selecting your logo, remember that it will need to last you for many years, so don't choose something that will date quickly. You should also select a design that will photocopy and fax well, and that will look effective in black as well as in colour. If you use computers and desk top publishing, consider a logo that will scan and print out well, so that you can drop it into documents, onto typed invoices, and use it in other ways via your computer, thus giving everything that you produce your corporate identity. (A scanner is a machine that turns an image on the page into an image on your computer, by converting it into dots which your computer can reproduce. If you don't have a scanner, you can get your logo scanned onto disk at most High Street printers for just a few pounds or your designer can do it for you.)

Don't get carried away with lots of colours for your logo, as it will be far too costly for you to implement. Think what your printing bills for your stationery would be if you were to opt for a multi-colour logo. A talented designer will be able to do something attractive and creative with just one or two colours, plus tints. If you get a two colour logo that uses soft pastels or light shades, you may still end up having to have a third colour for printing text, as you will find that the colours used in your logo are too light to work effectively for text in leaflets and publications, or even on your letterhead. You will probably need to add black for text.

When looking for a designer to help you with a new logo, the same rules apply as when choosing and using a designer for any other project (see above).

But why bother with a logo at all? Because it can be a powerful way of representing visually what your organisation is about. If you don't believe me, just think about the swastika, which is, after all, just a logo. It evokes strong feelings and emotions, it conjures up painful images, it affects and distresses people. Your logo will not do this in the same way, because the events and images associated with your organisation will be quite different. The swastika example is used merely to demonstrate how a symbol can be instantly recognisable and emotive. Your logo can do this in a more positive, albeit smaller, way. You can use it to convey what you do, to create appeal, to move people, to attract attention. The logo has many uses, so it is worth investing in one, and being clear at the outset how you are going to use it, and what you hope to get out of it, so that you can brief your designer.

A final word about logos – when presented with a choice of designs, opt either for the one you like most, regardless of whether it encapsulates a particular meaning, or go for one that visually represents your work. Don't choose anything where the meaning is so subtle that it requires a separate leaflet to explain it! Some proud designers write pretentious prose to explain what their random geometric shapes symbolise, and too many clients get taken in. If you're told that the shapes before you are a visualisation of caring, commitment and professionalism, but to you they look like an upturned turtle, trust your instincts and opt for another design.

STRAPLINES

A strapline is a statement or description which is used in conjunction with an organisation's name. Here are some fictitious examples:

■ Pedal Power: Fighting For Cyclists' Rights

■ Brunswick City Council: Improving Services, Creating Jobs

■ Jeremy's Furniture Emporium: The Best Furniture For Less

■ Head First: The National Charity For Brain Injured People

The idea is to use a strapline to explain a name that is not self-explanatory (such as Head First) or to emphasise a philosophy or commitment. The strapline is then used as part of the design on stationery and publications, in conjunction with your logo.

THE JARGON GUIDE

CALL-OUT: A short extract from the main text, which is repeated as a sub-head within the text, in order to draw attention to it.

GSM: Paper is referred to by designers and printers according to its weight. Typical notepaper is around 100gsm, or grammes per square metre. Magazine covers are much heavier, weighing in at around 220gsm.

INITIAL CAPS: This is where a word is in lower case letters, but the first letter uses a capital, such as England or Denise.

JUSTIFIED TEXT: Justified text produces lines of text of equal length. Unjustified text has a distinctive ragged or uneven right hand margin.

PICTURE LIBRARY: This is a commercial library containing thousands of photographs which cover every conceivable subject. You can borrow photos and use them, as long as you pay a fee and acknowledge the photographer or picture library in your credits. If you need a special picture, your designer should be able to track it down for you through a library. (See section on photography for further information.)

POINT SIZE: Typefaces are measured in points. Most books, magazines and letters are typed in 10 or 12 points. The larger the number, the larger the type size.

REVERSED OUT: This term describes the process by which the image or words themselves are not printed, but the surrounding area is. The text or image thereby appears to take on the colour of the paper.

TINTS: These are made up of tiny dots which give the effect of a shade. If you are printing in dark blue, your tints would be in shades of lighter blue. For black ink, tints are grey, for red ink they are pink. Effective use of tints can give the illusion of another colour.

UPPER CASE: Capital letters.

NAMING NAMES

But talking of names, what's in a name? Quite a lot. Just think about people's names and what you assume about them on the basis of what they are called, before you've even met. Do you think that Leeroy Winston Garvey would have much in common with Mr. and Mrs. Archibald and Gladys Wilkins? Or with Miss Vanessa D'Arcy-Windsor? People will judge your organisation by its name, so using terms in your title such as crippled, spastic, coloured people, the deaf, the blind etc. will say something about your outlook. You might be seen as old-fashioned, paternalistic, do-gooders if you pick the wrong name.

But what do you do if you came up with your name many years ago, you know it's no longer suitable or acceptable, yet it is now so well known that you take a risk if you change it? Take comfort in the fact that other organisations have changed theirs successfully. The Marriage Guidance Council changed to Relate in recognition of the fact that many long term relationships now take place out of marriage, with co-habitation being much more common now than when the organisation was founded.

The National Council for Civil Liberties switched to the snappier and more popular Liberty. Many others have done it too. If your name is a turn-off or it's no longer suitable for whatever reason, do consider changing it, and regard the renaming as an opportunity for publicity and a focus for fundraising or support-building. Combine it with a whole new identity and embark on a drive to publicise the change, explain it, and reach new audiences (without alienating your existing supporters).

GETTING INTO PRINT

Unlike designers, printers have a rough and ready image. Nevertheless, many people are just as cautious about talking to printers as to designers, mainly because they don't understand the print production process, they are unfamiliar with the jargon and afraid of being made to look foolish. Dealing with printers is easy, once you've found a good one.

Never open Yellow Pages, select a printer, and book them for your job – unless you have money to waste. Printers' prices vary enormously, so always shop around and get at least three quotations. Let your printers

> **TRUE STORY**
>
> There is something called 'nominative determinism', a subconscious force that makes a person gravitate to a job which fits his or her surname. To prove it, here are some real life examples:
>
> J. Lust, a sex therapist
> D. Weedon, author of a paper on incontinence
> D. Snowman, author of a book on the North Pole
> Miss Satchel, a school teacher
> I'm still waiting to meet a dentist called Phil McCaverty!!

> **TIP**
>
> *The copy you supply your typesetter needs to be typed into a machine before it can be typeset. As nearly all organisations now use word processors, you can often save money by handing over your copy on a disk, so that it doesn't have to be re-typed. Check first, however, as your disk will need to be compatible with your typesetter's, and will need to arrive in the right format.*

know that you are seeking other quotes, so that they come back to you with a more competitive price than they might otherwise offer. Small, local printers are often cheaper than the High Street quick-print shops. If you use a printer often, you should be able to negotiate a special rate or discount. Even if you are just an occasional user, consider joining forces with other organisations in your area to see if together you can get a bulk deal. And remember that high prices do not always mean high quality.

Ensure that you give a written specification to each printer, so that you can compare like with like. Check that your quotations include extras such as folding, delivery and corrections. Agree a timetable for the job and confirm this in writing.

Many printers also do typesetting, so it's worth asking. If not, they can usually recommend a typesetter, as can your designer.

BRIEFING PRINTERS

Just as a designer needs a brief, so too does a printer. If you are using a designer to get your material produced, they may offer to deal with the printer for you, which can be useful. Check first, however, that they will not add a mark-up to their bill for doing this. Some designers include a quote for print as part of their estimate. They then pay the printing costs and invoice you for design and print, and while this all sounds very straightforward, it can work out more expensive. It is standard practice for designers (and PR consultants) to add an extra 17% to printing costs, so be clear on this before you go ahead, and if necessary do your own print-buying.

When getting quotes from printers you will need to tell them:

■ **PRINT RUN**: how many copies you need. A run-on (extra copies done at the same time) is much cheaper than a reprint (extra copies done at a later date), so if you are in doubt about how many you need, opt for a few extra, as this could save you considerable money in the long run. It is not economical to get small amounts (generally under 400) printed; photocopying might be a better option

■ **COLOURS**: for the inks (if you are unsure, ask to see the Pantone book – see Jargon Guide for an explanation) and the paper (ask your printer to show you samples)

■ **PAPER**: the type, weight, size and colour

- **SIZE**: of paper and document (dimensions of page and number of pages)

- **OTHER**: other requirements, such as finishing (folding, stapling and stitching, for example), delivery, VAT

Full colour printing is, obviously, much more costly than just one or two colours. Having an A4 sheet folded will also put up the price, as will having documents stapled, or using non-standard size paper. Both your designer and printer can advise you on the cost implications of doing fancy things with your publications.

The main thing is not to be seduced into using lots of colours. As well as being costly, this can appear too lavish. By investing in clever design, it is possible to produce really attractive two-colour leaflets.

THE JARGON GUIDE

COLOUR-SEPARATED CAMERA READY ARTWORK: This is artwork that arrives in a form ready for printers to process. The original colours have been separated using special filters.

FINISHING: This is the final stage of the print production process, where the document is made ready for use by, for example, being cut, stitched, glued or guillotined.

FULL COLOUR PRINTING: This is produced using the four colour process. Your designs are split into their four original colours, yellow, magenta (red), cyan (blue) and black, using special filters. This is known as colour separation.

HALFTONES: This is a photograph which has been 'scanned' or 'screened' by a printer to turn it into a series of different sized dots which give the appearance of a continuous tone.

PANTONE COLOUR: There are many different shades of the same colour, so in order to ensure consistency, designers and printers use something known as the Pantone Matching System (PMS). Every shade has a Pantone number to identify it.

CHAPTER EIGHT

CAMPAIGNING

Increasingly, charities and voluntary organisations are having to take on campaigning work – to highlight local problems such as homelessness, poverty, or lack of facilities, or to lobby for more funding. This chapter will show you how to mount a successful campaign and how to avoid the pitfalls.

Well-planned campaigns carried out by experienced campaigners can produce startling results, raising awareness and helping to bring about change. There is no substitute for experience when it comes to campaigning, but the following information will help you if you are new to this field. Follow the tips and talk to other campaigners. Pick their brains and ask for advice. And finally, make sure that you are not, and never become, guilty of the seven deadly sins of campaigning:

SEVEN ROUTES TO A QUICK DOWNFALL

1. **Being vague about what you are trying to achieve**. Always be absolutely clear about your aims and objectives. Write them down so that everyone has the same understanding of what you are working towards.

2. **Launching a campaign that is unnecessary**. If another organisation is successfully campaigning on the same issue, join forces, don't compete or duplicate. If there another way of achieving what you want, do that instead.

3. **Talking tommyrot**. Feeling strongly about an issue is important, but it's not enough. You need to do research and know what you are talking about. Gather together facts and figures to support your case.

4. **Being amateurish**. Whatever you do, do it well. Good presentation need not cost money and it will certainly help you to be taken seriously by others. So adopt a professional attitude at all times.

5. **Losing a sense of perspective or becoming fanatical**. However passionately you feel about the issue, try to speak in measured tones and keep your objectivity. That way, people will be more inclined to listen and to take notice.

6. **Engaging in internal power struggles and in-fighting.** Remember that you are all on the same side, so don't let your campaign fall apart though in-fighting. Keep your fire power for the real enemy, or you'll end up shooting yourself in the foot.

7. **Letting the morale of your supporters flag.** Whenever you achieve something, however small, let everyone know. It helps maintain interest and gives the impression that the campaign is going somewhere.

A tip for successful campaigning is, wherever possible, to involve those affected by the problem: a campaign for jobs should involve unemployed people, a campaign to combat discrimination against disabled people should not involve able-bodied people alone. It will give you a better insight into what you are doing as well as added credibility. It's also less paternalistic if you are working on equal terms with people you are trying to help.

It's also worth remembering that when presenting your case, you should try to put forward solutions to the problem. That way you are less likely to come across as grumbling, and more likely to be seen as constructive and forward-looking. A Campaign *For* Homes is better than a Campaign *Against* Homelessness.

Don't forget to use the skills of those in your campaign group. Carry out a 'skills audit' to discover what talent you have at your disposal. Ask your members if they have access to useful equipment such as photocopiers or desk top publishing computers. Perhaps you have a good amateur photographer among your ranks, or someone with artistic flair. Also use the skills of the family and friends of people in your campaign group.

A successful campaign relies upon good planning. If a campaign fails, it's because its aims were totally unrealistic, or, more likely, because it was poorly planned and badly executed. So **before** you launch, be clear about what you are doing and why.

CAMPAIGN PLANNING

By answering the following questions, you should have a better picture of what you want to achieve, what the potential problems are, and how you should approach your campaign.

- What do you want and why do you want it? (What are your short-term objectives? What do you want in the long term?)

- Who is your target? (Who is your campaign aimed at? Who are you trying to influence? Who are the decision-makers?)

■ What is most likely to influence them? What are their vulnerabilities? How can you exploit these?

■ Who are your opponents?

■ What are the weaknesses of your own case? What mud can the opposition sling at you, and how will you respond/protect yourself? Are there any weaknesses that you can turn into strengths?

■ What is your most likely source of support? How can you involve them in the campaign? Are you likely to alienate any areas of potential support by your approach to your campaign? Is there a way around this?

■ What aspects of your case are most likely to appeal to supporters? (Bear in mind that different aspects will appeal to different groups of supporters.)

■ What sort of campaign is most appropriate? A 'behind the scenes' campaign where you try to influence from within, or a public and media-based campaign?

■ Will you go for one big push and a blaze of publicity or a more drawn out campaign? Which will work best for you? Can you sustain interest in a long-running campaign?

■ Will your campaign have a name? What will it be? What about a logo and letterhead? Who will design it? What will it cost? (See previous chapter.)

■ How much will your whole campaign cost and where will you get the money from? How much money do you need now? How much can you get later on?

THE LAUNCH

If your campaign has an official launch, it will present your very best opportunity for getting publicity, discussing the issue you are campaigning on, and building support, so don't waste it. Good preparation and planning will help you get off to a flying start.

■ If your campaign is having an official launch, what form will it take? What will happen at it? (Stunt, press conference, party?)

■ Can you build up support before you launch your campaign?

■ Will you need to prepare any publicity materials for the launch? (Press packs, an exhibition, handouts, photographs, factsheets, letterheads, news release paper, badges, balloons.)

CAMPAIGN CASE STUDY
THE GOOD PRACTICE CAMPAIGN

Background:

General practitioners are allowed to remove patients from their practice list without giving a reason. Patients have no right to be told the reason nor to an appeal.

Why is a campaign necessary:

Under the current system there are too many opportunities for discrimination to take place (against black people, gays, people with particular medical conditions etc.) and for the most vulnerable to lose out. Patients' watchdogs recognise that there is a need for a change in the law, but with so many other issues to campaign on, this is not a priority.

Short-term objectives:

- To publicise the issue: most patients are unaware that they have no rights
- To build up support for the campaign in order to demonstrate that there is backing for new legislation

Long-term objectives:

To achieve a change in the legislation so that:

- GPs can only strike off a patient if their behaviour is unreasonable as defined in the legislation e.g. violent, aggressive or racially abusive
- Patients are told the reason why they are being removed
- Patients have the right to appeal to an independent arbitrator

Targets:

- The public – to inform them
- Health councils and other organisations – to get their support
- Sympathetic MPs – to get them to lobby the government
- The government – to get them to change the law

Most likely influencing tactics:

Persuade the government that such a change in legislation would be in harmony with the Patient's Charter and other government initiatives, and would support their argument that patients are consumers of healthcare services. Showing massive public support is also likely to influence.

Opponents:

- General practitioners
- The British Medical Association
- Many health authorities and health boards

Counter arguments:

- GPs need the strike off power to protect them from ever-demanding and hostile patients
- Having to give reasons to patients could place the doctor in a difficult or delicate position
- If the doctor/patient relationship has broken down, it is in the patient's best interest to find a new GP

Sources of support:

- Community health councils and other patients' organisations
- Organisations representing groups of people more likely to be struck off, e.g.:
  - mental health charities
  - homelessness groups
  - drug-user support groups
  - women's groups
  - home birth lobby groups
  - groups representing people with chronic health conditions

How can they be involved?

- ask them to publicise the issue in their newsletter
- get them to circulate a petition in their next mailing
- ask them to write letters of support to the campaign, to newspapers and to their MPs

Type of campaign:

Very much a public, media-based campaign with lots of contact with other groups. Some work behind the scenes in building up support. A launch with a blaze of publicity followed by on-going media coverage aimed at producing one mention each month.

Budget:

Money required for stationery and stamps. Letterhead produced in-house on computer. Raise money by writing articles on the campaign and asking supportive groups for donations.

The launch:

- Write a feature on the issue for The Scotsman, timed to appear on launch day. Put the £100 freelance fee for the story into the campaign kitty.
- Send out news releases to relevant publications including locals, nationals and medical press, plus TV and radio.
- Seek a 'comment' slot on Scottish national radio.
- Arrange an hour-long phone-in on Scottish national radio.
- Write to potential supporters asking for assistance.

Follow up:

- Go national, tying in with report being published in England and Wales on the same subject, issuing further news releases.
- Give TV and radio interviews and provide human interest case studies to media.
- Arrange meeting with sympathetic MPs and seek the support of the Shadow Health Spokesperson, as well as the other political parties.
- Give talks to sympathetic groups and encourage signature gathering for the petition.
- Issue one news release each month announcing new campaign supporters, to give the impression that the campaign is constantly growing.

- Who will organise the launch? Where will it take place? (Try to ensure that your launch does not clash with another event which might detract attention.)

- Who will you invite? (Supporters? Potential supporters? The media?)

- Can you draw up a campaign programme, listing a series of events planned for the first few days/weeks/months of the campaign?

This final point is crucial. Launching your campaign is important, but so too is sustaining interest in it. Many campaigns get off to a good start with a high profile launch, but they soon peter out. If your campaign is to run for any length of time, you need to plan the highlights well before launch day, and have them scheduled into a campaign programme.

When you get down to planning events, you will soon discover than there are limits to the number of ways in which you can present the same points. You will need to be really imaginative if you are to find enough different ways of saying the same thing.

Let's look at a fictitious example.........

A campaign for safer cycling on main roads wishes to publicise the hazards to cyclists in the area. Presenting the facts (e.g. number of injuries each year) should be straightforward, but what next? Here are some ideas:

- arrange a photocall – get campaign members to turn up with bandages, slings and crutches, to highlight the injuries cyclists receive

- organise a stunt – perhaps a game of 'pot-hole golf'

- announce names of important local people or organisations who have pledged support to your campaign – particularly people who are associated with cars, such as rally drivers or the AA

- get a petition going – announce the start of the petition, publicise how many signatories you have got to date, and have a photocall when you are ready to hand your petition over

A useful tip to help you sustain interest is to make sure that you don't release everything in one go. If you have two really interesting bits of information, do not announce them in one news release, but divide them between two, sent out with a few days between.

GETTING ORGANISED

If your campaign is big or will run for a long time, it's probably best to have a committee to run it. You'll need a chair, a secretary and a treasurer (who could double up as a fundraiser) and you might also benefit from a co-ordinator, a membership officer, a press and publicity officer and maybe even a president or patron (a celebrity or figurehead).

Once you get organised, your meetings will need to be properly organised too. You'll need to prepare agendas and stick to them, to take minutes and circulate them, and to keep on top of the inevitable correspondence and general paperwork that all of this generates. Even if your campaign group is informal, keeping notes and records is useful. So is a clear understanding of the roles and responsibilities of the individual members. Assigning titles such as 'fundraiser' or 'chair' to members gives them well-defined duties and ensures that jobs get done. You might want to go one stage further and produce job descriptions (even if your staff are unpaid!). It leaves everyone knowing exactly what is expected of them.

THE CAMPAIGNER'S TOOL KIT

Campaigners have many tools available, some of them expensive, but most cheap or even free. Some will be more appropriate than others, depending on your image, your budget and your campaign objectives. Take from your toolbox the tools or campaigning methods that are right for you. This campaigner's tool kit has been organised alphabetically:

A is for – ACTION: Ask people to participate in your campaign by taking some action themselves. Spell out what action they can take, and make it as easy as possible for them to do it.

B is for – BANNERS: Strategically placed banners are a good way of getting the message across. They are also handy for marches, sit-ins and vigils, as well as a host of other events. You can get banners made professionally (although this can be expensive) or you can make your own if you have skilled helpers. But if you can't do it well, don't bother.

BALLOONS: Getting balloons printed is not expensive, and it can be a fun way to spread the word. See Yellow Pages for details of companies specialising in this. Try looking under 'Promotional Goods' or similar. You will probably need to hire some helium canisters, as blowing up 500 balloons by mouth is hard work, even for the fittest pair of lungs!

BADGES: These have a long shelf-life and are fun to wear, but they can be expensive to produce. It is possible to hire a badge-making machine, or you could investigate whether your community centre or local art college have one. Make your badges attractive if you want people to wear them.

BOYCOTTS: Boycotting campaigns have had tremendous success in attracting attention and putting pressure on companies to change their practices. The boycotts of South African produce or banks such as

Barclays, with major interests in that country, were influential in helping change the situation there, if only in a minor way.

C is for – CAR STICKERS: These are a good way of reaching a great many people. When you are stuck in a traffic jam or at traffic lights, don't you read the stickers on the car in front? If you can, choose wording that is appropriate to the situation – the National Blood Transfusion Service produce car stickers which say "I'm a blood donor. Drive safely or you might need me." A petrol company have stickers which say "If you can read this then you're driving too close."

COALITIONS: Forming a coalition with other interested organisations and groups will enable you to present a united front and to show the strength of support for your cause.

D is for – DEPUTATIONS: Sending a deputation to talk to decision-makers can be a way of getting some media attention and encouraging the other side to listen to your case.

E is for – ENGINEERING: Sometimes you have to 'engineer' or set things up that would not otherwise happen, such as a photocall or stunt. If you base your campaign around events that happen naturally, you may get nowhere. Often you must create your own news.

F is for – FORGING LINKS: Links and alliances with other campaigns in this country and abroad is a good way of sharing ideas and information, and building a more powerful movement.

G is for – GIMMICKS AND STUNTS: Use these to attract attention, from passers-by and from the media. If you are planning a stunt and you want media coverage, send out a media invitation to reporters and photographers.

H is for – HUMOUR: You can introduce humour into your campaign sometimes, even with quite serious subjects. It can be a good way of making your work less threatening to potential, but wavering, supporters.

I is for – INFORMATION: Get as much information as you can and use it as a weapon, both to support your cause and to undermine the opposition.

J is for – JOINING FORCES: Forming partnerships with similar organisations and campaigns can make you a much stronger force, more likely to be taken seriously.

K is for – KIDS: Children and animals have appeal, so if you can involve them in your campaign, do so. Some would call it shameless exploitation, others would say it's about using your assets. A photo of a child holding a placard with 'Save my School' splashed across it holds more appeal to the general public (and newspaper editors) than teachers on a march carrying banners printed with 'Stop the Education Cuts.'

L is for – LOBBYING: It is your MP's job to represent you, so don't hesitate to lobby them, to try to influence them, and to win their support. Big pressure groups employ professional parliamentary lobbyists, but you can do it yourself. Write to your MP, attend one of their surgeries, or phone them at the House of Commons (tel. 0171 219 3000), where you will be able to talk to their secretary or researcher. Arrange to see them either in London or in their constituency. After a meeting with your MP, ask them what they intend to do (your MP will be able to explain the many ways in which they can help, including asking parliamentary questions, signing early day motions, and supporting adjournment debates). Contact your MP afterwards to see whether they have taken any action yet. Keep up the pressure. You can also lobby your Euro MP (your MEP) and your local councillors.

LEAFLETS: When producing a campaign leaflet, refer to the chapter on publications for tips and information.

M is for – MEDIA COVERAGE: See the chapter on using the media to find out more.

N is for – NEWSLETTERS: Keep supporters informed of campaign achievements and other news, so they don't lose interest or lose touch. Use newsletters to inform potential supporters and encourage them to join the cause.

O is for – ORATOR: Whether they're at Speakers' Corner or on a soapbox in Sunderland, a good orator will be invaluable to your campaign, to act as media spokesperson, to address meetings, and to rally support.

P is for – PETITIONS: They must include addresses and signatures if they are to be valid.

POSTERS: Never put too much copy on a poster; it will not be read. Remember that flyposting is illegal.

PHOTOCALLS: If you have a story that could make a good picture (perhaps it involves children, cute animals, or something else that would make an eye-catching photograph) arrange a photocall.

PUBLIC MEETINGS: If these are to be worth the effort, they need to be well attended, and therefore to be well publicised. Choose a venue that is easy to get to, and lay on transport for people who are elderly or disabled. Aim for a venue that is wheelchair accessible, perhaps with an induction loop for deaf people. Consider having a crèche. Time your meeting to suit your target audience. Meetings at 'official' buildings such as town halls tend to attract only activists, as many ordinary people are wary of entering large municipal venues. Consider using a community centre instead and remember to decorate it with your publicity. It's a good trick to book a room that is slightly smaller than you need. You should also put out fewer chairs than you think you'll use, so that your helpers have to put out extra as people arrive. By doing these two things, you will give your audience the impression that the meeting has been much more successful than you hoped. A large, half empty room containing 20 people signals failure. A small, packed room with 20 people is a success!

Q is for – QUESTIONNAIRES AND SURVEYS: These are useful for backing up your claims, demonstrating support and attracting media coverage.

R is for – RALLIES, MARCHES AND DEMONSTRATIONS: Rallies, marches and demonstrations can be a good way of pulling together your supporters, making them feel a sense of unity and togetherness, and giving them a sense of achievement, but beware. They can alienate a lot of potential supporters who regard marches as aggressive and disruptive. If you are planning a march, make sure you get permission from the police first.

RECRUITMENT: The more members you have, the more likely you are to be successful. Set each of your members a target to recruit new people to the campaign. Even if the target is just one, you can double the size of your campaign. Don't miss recruitment opportunities, such as at your public meetings or when you are asking people to sign your petition.

S is for – SIT-INS: Sit-ins are a way of attracting attention, but they may lose you support if you are seen as being aggressive, and they may be illegal.

STALLS: Setting up an information stall in your town centre on a busy Saturday can attract both attention and support for your campaign.

SLOGANS: Try to come up with a catchy or clever slogan that summarises what your campaign is about.

T is for – TALKS AND PRESENTATIONS TO OTHER ORGANISATIONS: These are a good way of spreading the word and winning support. Make sure that your speaker is confident and knowledgeable, or they could do more harm than good. Try to use visual aids such as slides, videos or overheads to brighten up the presentation and to help get your message across. Never read from a script – use notes by all means, but aim for a natural delivery or you will send your audience to sleep. Don't forget to take your publicity material along to hand out, and a sheet of paper for potential supporters to leave their details on.

T-SHIRTS: Spread the message by wearing it across your chest! Many of the bigger pressure groups produce 'designer' T-shirts, which are now being worn as a fashion accessory by people who have little idea of the work of the group they are publicising in this way. Getting

T-shirts printed is not expensive, or you can buy cheap, plain white T-shirts and decorate your own using fabric paints. For short runs, it's cheaper to opt for laser transfer printing, but screen printing is more cost-effective if you want a larger number produced.

U is for – UNDERCOVER: Turn spy and find out what the opposition are up to. Send off for their publicity materials, attend their meetings, write to them for information, get to know what their plans are.

V is for – VIGILS: Vigils are often better options than sit-ins; candlelit vigils exude a more peaceful air.

VIDEOS: Thanks to community video resource centres, which are available in many towns and cities, campaign groups can now produce semi-professional videos, which can be an efficient way of taking the message to the people. You can show a video in place of, or in support of, a speaker. They can liven up talks and presentations you are doing for potential supporters. (See chapter on video.)

W is for – WRITING LETTERS: Letters to newspapers are a good way of reaching a large number of people for the price of a stamp. Don't send the same letter to all newspapers; write different ones for each, and make them appropriate to the audience. If you are organising a writing campaign to MPs or councillors, get your campaign members to write personal letters, rather than simply sending a standard photocopied letter.

WORD OF MOUTH: It's the cheapest way of letting people know about your work.

X is for – XCITEMENT! (Yes I know it's not spelt like that.) Making campaigning exciting and fun is crucial if you want to maintain the interest of your supporters. Even serious campaigns should have an element of the exciting, or even just the social. Meeting for a cup of coffee, holding a celebration over a minor victory – it's all important for keeping morale up.

Y is for – YARDSTICK: If your campaign seeks to influence opinion, you might need to carry out some initial research before you launch. This will enable you to measure your success and will provide you with a media opportunity to demonstrate it – you could issue something like: "Thanks to the Save a Sea Fish Campaign, 50% more adults are aware of the dangers to sea fish of disposable nappies, sanitary products and bleached loo roll."

Z is for – ZANY: Mad things, when and where appropriate, can help get your campaign attention. One man was having a dispute with his local council and he had frequently accused them of sticking their heads in the sand over the issue. Eventually in frustration he attended a council meeting dressed as an ostrich, much to the embarrassment of councillors and the delight of press photographers. The element of humour in his stunt help win him public support and showed the council up as a stuffy, bureaucratic and humourless organisation.

...add other tools as you need them.

The key is to go for variety, to be creative but not to overlook tried and tested methods, and to involve radio and TV as well as the local press, if appropriate. Do all of this, get your planning right, and you have the makings of a successful campaign.

SWELLING THE CAMPAIGN COFFERS:
A Guide to Fundraising

Campaigns can be run on a shoestring, but you'll probably need some money and possibly more than you think. Start by listing what you'll need to spend money on, so that you have a budget and a clear picture of where the money will go. Next work out how much you need and by when. Finally, appoint a treasurer and fundraising committee, put your thinking caps on, and come up with money-making ideas.

Jumble sales and car boot sales might not be glamorous, but they are great ways of getting money. Other ideas include:

- collections at public meetings
- donations from individuals and groups
- corporate donations and sponsorship
- grants from other charities and trusts
- sponsored events such as a sponsored silence
- social events such as a disco or dinner
- fairs and fêtes
- auctions
- sale of campaign materials such as fact sheets and booklets
- special campaign merchandise such as T-shirts and mugs (the risk here is that an initial outlay is required and there is always the danger that you might not recoup it all, let alone make a profit)
- flag days and door-to-door collections (you will need official permission and identification badges)

The laws governing charity fundraising are complex and it's best to seek advice before holding anything likely to require permission or compliance with regulations, such as a lottery, street collection or competition. Your local council for voluntary service should be able to point you in the right direction.

WHAT'S IN A NAME?

Finding an apt, short and snappy name for your campaign will help you no end. It needs to be something appropriate and memorable. A good example is the campaign aimed at boycotting toys from China made using child labour; it was called Toycott.

Acronyms are useful if you can't think of a one or two-word name. At university we had a campaign called CRAP (Campaign for Real Andrex Paper)! Remember that an acronym should be pronounceable.

TALKING POLITICS

There are rules and regulations which govern charities when it comes to campaigning and actions which could be considered political. If you want to check that your planned campaign is not in breach of the regulations, contact the Charity Commission for guidance (0171 210 4477, London office; 0151 703 1500, Liverpool office; 01823 345000, Taunton office) or talk to your local council for voluntary service.

The Charity Commission highlights the following as examples of activities in which charities should not engage:

■ they must not seek to influence public opinion or put pressure on the government, either directly or indirectly through their supporters, to legislate or to adopt a particular policy on the basis of slanted or inaccurate data

■ they should not participate in party political demonstrations or conduct publicity campaigns indicating how individual MPs or parties voted on a particular issue as a means of applying public pressure on those MPs or the government

■ they must not provide supporters or the public with pro forma letters to send to MPs or the government

■ they must not produce publicity material which is biased

■ a charity which publishes the results of research must not manipulate the information so as to present a partial view to support a preconceived position or objective

There are many other things you are not allowed to do if you are a charity, so always check first to avoid landing yourself in trouble.

HAVE A GO YOURSELF

Put on your thinking caps and have a go at being creative with the following campaigns.

CAMPAIGN ONE

You live in Redford, a 1930s housing estate. There is an old-style red telephone box on the estate, which costs British Telecom more in maintenance than they make in profits at that particular box. They therefore plan to remove the red telephone box and to replace it with a modern, vandal-proof kiosk.

You want the red phone box to remain, and you are about to mount a campaign, along with 100 other residents, to get it saved. Ultimately you plan to get the phone box designated a listed building, but BT plans to remove in it two weeks, and listing will take longer than that.

Find a name for your campaign and come up with a series of events, stunts, photocalls and anything else to attract attention and to put pressure on BT to give your callbox a reprieve. You have no money in the campaign coffers, but you can embark on fundraising if you wish. Remember your deadline, though.

CAMPAIGN TWO

You are a member of a local road safety campaign in Potterston. A busy main road in your town, one which runs near a primary school, has no safe crossing place, and six pedestrians have been killed on the road in the last three years, three of them children. The highways department has been asked by parents of children at the school to install a pelican crossing, but they have been told that this cannot be done for another 12 months, as there is no money left in the budget.

You want a crossing to be installed immediately, before there is another accident. You have only £10 in the kitty.

Find a name for your campaign, list who you will approach for support, and come up with publicity-attracting events that will help you get your message accross.

In planning these two campaigns you will have discovered that campaign planning is difficult, yet good fun, even for serious campaigns. It offers an opportunity to be creative and to find many ways of getting the same message across.

What did you come up with for Campaign One? How about this:

KEEP REDFORD RED

As a first step to getting some publicity and raising funds at the same time, organise a BT Boycott Day. Ask Redford residents to donate to campaign funds the money they would have spent on phone calls that day. Get publicity for your stunt in the local paper. (See Chapter 3 for details of how to do this.)

- Have a sit-in at the phone box, attracting attention and preventing it from being used. Organise a photocall for your sit-in, and get banners made to decorate the kiosk with.

- Hold sit-ins at main telephones in the town centre for one hour, and hand out leaflets to people seeking to use the phone you are occupying. Get them to sign your petition. Get your supporters to dress from top to tail in red.

- Persuade your local paper to run a small feature on the history of the red telephone box.

- Get local radio along. Your story has great radio potential for telephone sound effects.

- Jam BT's switchboard with calls complaining about their intentions in Redford.

That should be plenty to keep a campaign going for two weeks!

POTTERSTON NEEDS A PELICAN

Possible supporters include the parents of children at the local school, the children themselves, teachers and other staff, local businesses, relatives and friends of people killed and injured on the road, your local councillors, your MP, other road safety groups, the police road safety department, local nurseries and parent and toddler groups.

- You could do the usual things, such as a petition demanding immediate action.

- The schoolchildren could use face paints to make themselves up as pelicans and zebras, to highlight the need for a pelican or zebra crossing. This could form the basis for a photocall.

- You could sensitively approach one of the parents of a child killed on the road, and ask him/her to talk to the local paper or TV station, to show a human angle to the campaign.

- On the basis of past figures, you can say that another child and one adult will die on the road before the new crossing is installed. This could be issued as a news release, to bring home the story to local people.

- You could blockade the road for an hour as a publicity stunt.

- You could line the road with banners and placards, perhaps listing the names and ages of people who have been injured there.

- During the night, when the road is less busy, you could chalk a zebra crossing on the road, and place some mock pelican lights there, as a photocall stunt.

Some stunts are illegal (such as blockading roads) but if there is local sympathy for your cause the police may turn a blind eye unless they receive an official complaint.

CHAPTER NINE

PHOTOGRAPHY

There's more to using photographs than just getting them taken. Find out in this chapter how to commission a photographer, how to write a brief, how to use a photo library, and how to make best use of your photos.

Charities are making more and better use of photography these days, but it is still amazing to discover how many spend money on getting quality photographs taken, and then never make full use of them. If you invest in good photographs, make sure they work for you. Some ideas for using your photographs include:

- **EXHIBITIONS** – use your photographs to make up exhibition boards of your work, for display in your reception, or the local library or community centre

- **TALKS** – use slides to brighten up talks you are giving, and to help bring your work to life for the audience

- **THANK YOUs** – if you take pictures at events, it's nice to send copies to principal guests

- **PUBLICATIONS** – use your photos in leaflets and your annual report

- **NEWSPAPERS** – send appropriate photos to accompany news releases. (Make sure they are captioned, as they may get separated from your release. Newspapers prefer 8" x 6" pictures. Always send them in card-backed envelopes, as creased pictures are useless)

- **DECORATION** – mount your best photos and get them framed, for display in your reception or committee rooms

- **INDUCTION** – use slides for showing at staff training and induction sessions

IN THE PICTURE

But for organisations new to photography, how do you go about building up a photo library? Beware the keen amateur! The first step is to find a good professional photographer. Ask around, and if you get stuck, contact the picture editor of your local newspaper and ask them to recommend an affordable and reliable freelance. Or you could try the

TIP

Some photographers charge a small attendance fee, and make their money from selling you prints. Others charge a higher fee, but their prints are very reasonably priced. Find out the likely full cost of the job, and pick the photographer who will be most cost-effective for your requirements.

British Institute of Professional Photography (Tel. 01920 464011). They have members the length and breadth of the country, and can help you locate a photographer who is qualified.

Look at their portfolio to see what you think of their work. Good action photographers are not necessarily good people photographers, so you might need to use different people, depending on the assignment.

Having found your photographer, you need to provide a brief, which will include:

- a description of the photographic assignment – including dates and how long it will take

- full details of names, addresses etc. to be visited by the photographer, along with a schedule

- an idea of what you plan to do with the photographs/how you intend to use them

- whether colour or black and white is required (or both) – remember that you can now get decent black and white prints from colour negatives, but if you opt for black and white prints, that's what you are stuck with; they cannot be magically transformed into colour

- whether you want prints, slides or transparencies

You can include a brief as part of your letter confirming the booking. It might look something like the letter opposite.

Deciding whether to go for prints, slides or transparencies (photographers will refer to them as 'trannies') can be difficult, as each has plus and minus points. Slides are much more versatile, though they do cost more. If you give lots of presentations, opt for slides. Prints can be made into slides, but it's very expensive. Slides are easier to store, but prints are easier to view (you don't have the hassle of setting up a light box or projector). The drawback with prints is that they are not as hardy, and are more prone to damage. Transparencies are like larger format slides, but without the plastic mount. They are often favoured by designers and printers, and by magazines, but are less usable than slides and prints.

Try to be creative when it comes to photography. Pictures of committees sitting around a table, of directors shaking hands with worthies, or group shots of staff, are a bore. Not all photographers are imaginative, so don't rely on yours to come up with an interesting idea. If you see in newspapers and magazines photographs you like, cut them out and keep them. You can then show them to your photographer as an

East End Asian Youth

181 Howard Street, Templeton
Tel. 67113

Toby Wilson, Photographer
78 Nelson Mandela Way
Templeton

May 1st 1999

Dear Toby,

A note to confirm our booking and to give you further details of the brief we discussed on the telephone today.

We require black and white photographs for our annual report (see enclosed copy of last year's report). The final prints are required no later than July 1st, so we would need to see a contact sheet by mid-June. This will allow you sufficient time to get prints made up and delivered to us before our deadline.

As we explained to you, the images of Asian youth we see are so often stereotyped, and it is our aim to challenge some of these stereotypes through the photos in our report. The photos will also be used at a later date in an exhibition we are planning.

The shoot should take just over half a day, starting at 9am and finishing at around 2pm (see enclosed schedule). Asha Hussein will accompany you, provide transport and introduce you to those being photographed. You should meet her at our office on May 31st at 9am.

As agreed, your fee will be £200 inclusive, to cover your time, materials and expenses. We will pay additionally £4 per 6x8 black and white print ordered. Payment will be made on receipt of final prints.

Please contact me if you have any queries. Otherwise, Asha will see you here on the 31st.

Yours sincerely,

Asuk Ali
Co-ordinator

East End Asian Youth

181 Howard Street, Templeton
Tel. 67113

ASSIGNMENT

Black and white photographs for annual report

DATE

May 31st

SCHEDULE

9am Meet Asha Hussein at 181 Howard Street

9.30am Arrive at Templeton Football Club, Bedford Grove

Photograph Asian Girls' Under 18s Football Team

We are seeking in this picture to challenge the view that Asian girls are passive, have no freedom, and no life beyond the home.

We would like an action shot rather than a static group portrait.

11.00am Arrive at Abdul's Pizza Parlour, 12 High Street

Photograph Abdul making a pizza. We're looking for an arty shot, perhaps taken from an interesting angle, something that will make a striking picture. We aim to show that Asian Youth don't always work in Indian restaurants. Some set up their own businesses serving quite different food.

12.00pm Arrive at Jinny Singh's Interior Design Consultancy,
Granton House, 179 Townhouse Street

Jinny imports raw silks which she uses lavishly in her business.

Photograph Jinny showing one of her clients (we have made the arrangements for a client to be present) some bales of silk. We are looking here for a photograph that conveys the up-market image of Jinny's business. We intend to use this as our cover shot, if the picture is strong enough.

1.00pm Sandwiches in car *en route* to Templeton Swim Centre.

Photograph Sayed Uddin, the pool attendant/life guard. We would like a picture of him diving from the diving board into the deep end.

2.00pm The session will end at around 2pm. You will be returned to Howard Street to collect your car.

example of the sort of thing you are looking for; this can be easier than trying to describe it.

Think carefully about the images you are commissioning, as they should reflect the values of your organisation. See the specimen photographic brief at the end of this chapter for an example of how to write a brief and how to explain to a photographer which images you are seeking and which you wish to avoid.

You should always try to anticipate your photographic needs, in order to maximise the value of your photographic budget. If you commission a photographer to take some pictures for your annual report, and you know that two months later you will be producing your newsletter or a leaflet, get the photos for that taken at the same time.

Catalogue your photos so that you know what they show, when they were taken and by whom. And don't forget to ask your photographer for the negatives, so that you can get prints made up by a photographic lab if necessary, which could work out cheaper or easier for you.

> **TIP**
>
> *While you have a photographer working on an assignment for you, get him or her to take some black and white head and shoulders shots of your key staff. These are useful for popping into press packs, and will not add much to your bill if the photographer is working for you in any case.*

HOW TO COMPARE PRICES OF DIFFERENT PHOTOGRAPHERS

When you are shopping around for a photographer, you need to find out what they charge for:

- **attending your event** – some charge hourly and others charge a session rate, which is a day or half day

- **materials** – find out what they will bill you for and whether you will be charged at cost price

- **prints, slides and transparencies** – colour and black and white

- **contact sheets** – these are like very small prints, but they are all printed on one large sheet of photographic paper, enabling you to view the prints in miniature, before selecting those you want made up full size

- **expenses** – find out what you will get billed for (including the mileage rate, and whether you will be charged travelling time)

Using a picture library

A picture library is a library which has photographs instead of books. You pay a fee to use one or more of its photographs, and this can sometimes work out cheaper than commissioning your own original photography, if you are looking for something very special. Picture libraries can give you access to an enormous range of images, to the world's very best photographers, to photographs taken in faraway locations, to pictures using special effects and so on. So if you need a top quality picture of a woman dyeing cloth in Bangladesh, and commissioning your own would be impossible, contact a picture library.

Using a library is easy. You ring up and describe the kind of picture you are looking for, and they will either locate something suitable (generally they will come up with more than one picture), or suggest that you come in and have a look yourself. If you ask the library to find the image you are after, they may charge you a search fee (anything from around £20 up to £35), though this is usually waived if you then decide to buy the picture.

The cost of buying a picture varies enormously, depending on which library you use, how you intend to use the picture (for a slide presentation or in a brochure, for example), what the circulation will be, whether it will appear on the front cover or an inside page, how large it will be and so on. Generally the fee you pay is for a one-off use; you do not buy the rights to the photo.

When you are briefing a picture library, try to be as specific as possible about the kind of picture you have in mind. Don't just ask for a photo of someone in a wheelchair, as this raises too many questions, such as: male or female? what age? what ethnic origin? in a kitchen? outside? summer or winter? a positive, powerful image? a victim image? what era? 1950s? 1990s? colour?

Many libraries produce free catalogues, though they are not comprehensive; a catalogue can only show a fraction of a library's stock of tens of thousands (often millions) of images. Catalogues are useful, however, if you do not have a picture library near you and need to order by post.

There are general libraries with a wide range of images, and specialist ones, such as those specialising in scientific or nature photos, for example.

Across the country there are over 300 photo libraries (though the highest concentration is in the London area). To find out where they are, contact the British Association of Picture Libraries and Agencies (BAPLA) on 0181 444 7913.

THE JARGON GUIDE

CONTACT SHEETS: These are miniature prints which are reproduced in strips (rather like negatives) on a large sheet of photographic paper. They allow you to view and select your prints without the expense of getting them made up full size.

COPYRIGHT

Even when you have commissioned photography, you do not own the copyright, so when you buy the prints or transparencies from the photographer, that's all you're buying. Under the provisions of the Copyright, Designs and Patents Act 1988, copyright exists in all literary, musical, artistic and dramatic works, with the Act specifically including photography within the definition of an artistic work.

PHOTOGRAPHIC BRIEF

Introduction

The Granville People's Disabled Action Group wishes to add to its stock of photographs for use in its campaign and promotional material and in its monthly magazine, Disabled Action News. To achieve this, we wish to commission a photographer to provide us with photographs showing disabled people across Britain at work and play.

Approach

We wish to give our photographer a relatively free hand in deciding how best to undertake this commission. We have set out the main principles underlying the images which we wish to portray in our campaigning and promotional material, and these can be found in the section headed 'Specification'.

We have asked 20 of our member groups in different parts of the country for their co-operation with this project. The photographer would need to liaise with these organisations to make the necessary arrangements.

Requirements

We require the photographs to be supplied as colour transparency, two copies of each. The total number of photographs taken should be in the range of 800 to 1,200. The photographs should be ready by March 31 1995.

The photographs should be numbered and accompanied by a brief note of the subject matter, names of people pictured, and locality.

Copyright

We will own all photographs, although our photographer will be free to use the photographs (by seeking our permission, which we will freely grant provided this does not in any way prejudice the interests of the Granville People's Disabled Action Group).

Reference material

For reference and background information we have enclosed copies of recent campaign and promotional material.

Specification

We wish to project images which portray the positive and powerful side of disability. To this end, photographs taken should be in accordance with the following principles:

1. They should project strong, powerful, positive images.

2. Photographs should ensure that women are portrayed not only as mothers/wives, but as workers, managers and consumers.

3. Men should not be portrayed only in traditional roles.

4. Photographs should where possible portray the positive and active involvement of other disadvantaged and discriminated against groups (such as ethnic minorities and elderly people).

5. Photographs should avoid the use of traditionally negative and helpless images – e.g. dependent and pathetic people trapped in wheelchairs or on crutches.

6. Photographs should avoid the portrayal of disabled people being helped by able-bodied people.

7. Photographs should attempt to show the range of disabilities, including those which cannot be seen, such as deafness and visual impairment.

When a copyright owner (your photographer) authorises another person (your charity) to publish their work (in your annual report, for example), they are in effect granting a licence. This can be done orally, over the phone, for example, though it's always sensible to get something in writing too. Usually you need not worry too much about licences, as a licence is usually implied in that you are commissioning a photograph for a particular purpose. If, however, you go on to use the same photos in another publication, strictly speaking you should get another licence. It's unlikely that your photographer would actually require you to do this, though you should be aware of the possibility. If you want to be sure to avoid any such problems, get the copyright assigned to you (in writing) when you commission the photos.

CHAPTER TEN

EXHIBITIONS

Exhibitions offer a great opportunity for you to publicise your work. Most organisations have exhibited at least once, some with more success than others. This chapter will show you how to get the best out of exhibitions.

When people attend exhibitions they may visit many stands, but they take in no more than ten or twelve. Your aim in exhibiting is to ensure that yours is one of the memorable stands.

Achieving this involves getting your exhibition material right, getting your stand right, and getting your staff right. But before you get to the stage of planning this detail, you need to make a decision about whether or not to exhibit in the first place.

SETTING OBJECTIVES

Never exhibit simply because it seems like a good idea at the time. Always write down what you hope to achieve from exhibiting – your objectives – so that you can evaluate success. When considering taking a stand at an exhibition, ask: "What would we get out of it? Would this be justified in terms of the cost?" This will help you to decide whether or not to go ahead.

Your objectives might be to:

■ raise awareness of the charity among key decision-makers

■ sell copies of the new training manual

■ attract donations in the region of £1,000

If the exhibition is not likely to attract decision-makers and training managers, or your stand will cost more than the money you hope to make, you might decide against exhibiting at this particular event. But it's only by having a clear idea of what you hope to achieve that you can make an informed decision about whether or not to exhibit. You need to decide:

WHY – why exhibit? Is there a better way?

WHAT – what will we be exhibiting?

WHO – who will we be exhibiting to? Who will the audience be?

BENEFITS – what will we get out of it?

COST – how much is our budget? Can we do something to an acceptable standard for this budget? Is this the best way we can spend our publicity budget?

WHICH EXHIBITION?

Not all exhibitions are the same, so if you decide that exhibiting is for you, be careful to choose the right showcase. Select one that will enable you to reach your target audience, position you properly in terms of the image you are seeking, and that offers a cost-effective way of achieving these two objectives.

How do you know if you will be reaching the right audience? First of all decide who your audience(s) is, then ask the event organiser for an audience profile. This will provide you with a picture of who has attended the event in previous years and should also give you an idea of why they attended, what they hoped to get out of the event and so on. Reputable event organisers will produce an audience profile based on real research: if yours does not, perhaps you should consider finding a different and more professionally-organised event instead.

It is important that you are associated with a successful event, but its success will depend on its being properly set up and run. A good indication of this is whether the organisers have a clear PR and marketing strategy for promoting the event. Ask them questions about which media have been contacted about the event, whether features and coverage have been secured, about which journalists have been invited, who has attended in previous years and so on. Get them to show you media coverage from recent years. Ask also about mailings, whether fliers have been sent out and if so, how many and who to. Ask when, where and how the event will be advertised. Satisfy yourself that the organisers will work hard to draw in the target audience and to promote the exhibition.

Once you are sure that exhibiting is the right move, and that you have found an appropriate platform, it's time to think about your materials.

EXHIBITION BOARDS

If you are going to go to the trouble and expense of exhibiting, make sure that your material is up to scratch. If your boards look shabby and unattractive, no one will bother to come up to your stand, so your time and effort will have been wasted. Available budget plays a large part in the appearance of your exhibition material, but it's not the only factor, and it is possible to produce an attractive display without spending too much. You can use a designer or produce your exhibition boards in-house, depending on your budget and how important it is to get the exhibition looking really professional. Whether you're doing it yourself or using outside expertise, you will need to be clear on the following at the outset so that you can get the design and content right:

- Where will the exhibition be displayed? In a busy foyer or exhibition hall, or in a quiet library, for example. Your display site will affect the design.

- What exhibition display system will be used? A traditional display system such as Marler Hayley? (This is a manufacturer of modular exhibition boards. Other manufacturers make similar systems, which look good, are hard-wearing, lightweight and portable, and extremely versatile, but quite expensive. They can be hired.) Or card boards attached to a wall?

- Who will it be aimed at? Professionals? The public? Potential donors? Decision-makers? (Make sure the words and images are appropriate for the audience.)

- What are the key messages you want to get across? (Always keep it as simple as possible, preferably with just one clear message.)

Exhibitions are about visual impact, so don't get too bogged down with text, as no one will read it. Go for lots of bullet points to make the text quick to read and easy to digest, and try to represent as much as you can using graphics, charts, tables and photographs, with only small chunks of copy. Make your illustrations and text really large so they are easy to see and read, and make good use of your corporate identity on your boards. Don't forget lighting too. Will you need additional lighting for your display? How will you provide this?

Exhibition boards that can be chopped and changed are better than those that need to be shown in their entirety in order to make sense. If your panels work on their own, you have the basis for a much more flexible display. In a small space you can use only one or two of your boards.

If you have gone to the trouble of producing an exhibition for a particular event, try to find opportunities for displaying it again, perhaps in your reception or in your local community centre. Or consider lending it to other charities.

STAFFING YOUR EXHIBITION

It is always best to have staff standing at or near your display if you can. This provides you with an opportunity to answer questions and give further information to interested people. If your exhibition is going to be staffed, the seniority of staff should match the event. At a major conference, the staff on your stand should be fairly senior, confident in talking about your work, well-briefed and knowledgeable. If you are just handing out stickers, obviously there is no need for your director to be present.

Instruct staff to keep the stand (and themselves!) neat and tidy, with coffee cups well out of the way, because your organisation will be judged not just by the messages on your boards, but by your stand generally and by your staff. Don't let them huddle in groups laughing and chatting to each other. A professional approach is called for.

Be careful not to over-staff your stand, as this will put the punters off. They will feel out-numbered and reluctant to come over for fear of being pounced on. Staffing a stand is tiring, so fix up a rota and ensure that no one does more that three hours without a break. For an all-day exhibition attracting 10,000 people, an average sized stand requires three staff, two on duty and one available to relieve staff for their breaks, to free them to visit other stands and to take part in workshops.

To get the best out of exhibiting, staff should be fully briefed on what is expected of them, how they should handle enquiries, and on what you hope to get from the exhibition.

Staff should find the loos, café etc. before the doors open, as they are bound to be asked where these facilities are, and will foster more goodwill if they are able to help with instructions on how to find them.

ATTRACTING THE PUNTERS

However impressive or expensive your stand or display boards, they are useless if they fail to attract your target audience. Your aim when exhibiting is to get people across to look at your display, to talk to your staff, to pick up your literature, to put a few coins in your collection tin or a signature on your petition. There are various ways of attracting attention, but what you use depends on where you are exhibiting and who you are trying to attract.

> **TRUE STORY**
>
> Some people were collecting in the High Street for money to help save endangered whales. They were dressed in bee outfits, which made them look exceedingly stupid and caused confusion – were they collecting for bees or whales? Their gimmick was neither apt nor effective.

Essentially there are three types of punter: the 'committed', who will come up and take a look or pick up a leaflet out of genuine interest; the 'dead against', who has no interest in what you do and will not be enticed in; and the 'floating voter', who could be swayed to take a peek at your stand. The committed people are interested in any case, the 'dead againsts' will never develop an interest, so your challenge is to attract the 'floaters'.

When exhibiting at a big event, you need to make your display stand out from the many others. It's a bit like running a market stall in a marketplace that has 100 other stalls; yours needs to be eye-catching if it is to get the shoppers/visitors. However, you have the benefit of knowing that the people attending are doing so because they are interested in the issue. This cannot be said when you are staging an exhibition in the High Street on a Saturday afternoon. Passers-by are out to shop, not to look at displays, so a different tactic is required.

Start by thinking about who you want to attract, then devise a way of achieving this. For an exhibition stand aimed at parents in a busy shopping area, try getting your staff to dress up in Disney outfits to attract the children across, allowing you to talk to the parents. An exhibition for young people might do well with a small band performing at it, or pop music playing. Older people may be attracted by free cups of tea. Whatever gimmick you opt for, ensure that it is appropriate and will not reflect badly on you.

TRUE STORY

A computer software company was concerned that people visiting the exhibition hall would not be interested in its stand, when there were so many other interesting and eye-catching displays around. It decided to employ a caricaturist to get visitors up to the stand, and the tactic was extremely effective. Soon there was a long queue waiting for a free caricature. However, the punters soon disappeared with their free caricature, without lingering to look over the software. So remember that getting people to your stand is not enough, you need to get their attention turned to your work so that you can sell them your wares, be they ideas, a subscription, a covenant or a publication. Never use a gimmick to replace your message.

When you use a gimmick to get people over to your stand, ensure that you devise a gimmick that will attract the right people. There's no point in getting queues of punters at your stand if the majority of them are not interested in your work, but have come over for a freebie or to see a side-show.

Research has shown that stands which incorporate some activity or movement attract more visitors than those without this. A video or slide show, for example, are ideal, or even just a mobile swaying in the breeze. You aim is to ensure that your stand is not static and dull.

The biggest turn-off for people is a display area with no-one there other than staff. They are afraid to go up for fear of being nabbed by staff and forced to donate, join or support before they have had a chance to make up their own minds. Make sure your staff don't look as if they are hovering, ready to swoop on unsuspecting passers-by. When you do get to talk to visitors to your stand, never say "Can I help you?". People nearly always reply "No". Think of an opening line that is likely to produce conversation, not one that will kill it. Remember that your aim is to make visitors feel comfortable and at ease. That involves being sensitive to whether or not someone wants to talk, by watching their body language and looking out for other cues. Many people at exhibitions are paper-collectors; they pick up every possible leaflet and digest it all later on back at the office or at home. Leave these people alone when they visit your stand, and select others who look as if they are interested in talking.

Many exhibition organisers produce an exhibition catalogue. Think carefully about your entry in this, and ensure that the wording is designed to encourage people to seek out your stand. Make sure that the stand lives up to the description, or you will leave visitors feeling short-changed.

Never block the entrance to your stand with staff or tables, or make the entrance too narrow, thus making it difficult for people to get in. People don't want to have to negotiate an obstacle course to get to see your stand; if they have to, they will give up and spend their time at the stand next door instead.

Always have information for people to pick up and take away (such as your annual report and other publicity material), or freebies such as badges and balloons, and keep a pen and paper handy to take details from visitors who want further information about you. Better still, leave enquiry forms on your stand for visitors to complete. Always respond to enquiries as soon as you get back to the office, while the enquirer's interest and enthusiasm are still fresh.

YOUR STAND

Your exhibition stand is like a theatre; it is your stage and it is up to you to get the props, the actors and the play right. Decorate your stand in a style to suit. Put in seating if this is appropriate. Have some flowers on the table, or potted plants. Have some music playing in the background. Do everything you can to make your stand attractive, welcoming, and eye-catching. Screen a video if it will attract punters, or set out an attractive book display. Plan your stand so that it is easy for passers-by to stop and take a look or pick up a leaflet. If your stand is shabby, people will think your organisation is also.

> **TIP**
>
> *Having free coffee at your stand is often a good way of attracting people. The aroma brings them to your stand, and the hot coffee keeps them there, as long as you use real ceramic mugs and not paper cups – people will wander away with a paper cup, but not if they have a proper mug!*

THE COST OF EXHIBITING

A table and display in the local High Street will cost you nothing but time and energy, while a stand at an important international exhibition will set you back tens of thousands of pounds. You need to decide whether the cost will outweigh the benefits, and that involves setting objectives before you decide to take a stand.

At some venues you will be charged per square metre of space you occupy, or you may be given a space and told how big a display you can have on it. Some will charge you a premium for prime spots in the hall, while others will have a flat fee, so there will be a benefit in booking early and reserving the best site.

Generally when you are quoted a price for exhibiting, it will cover the space in the hall but anything else will be extra. There may be additional charges if you want a PA system, stand lighting, electricity, a video player or other equipment, so look into this carefully and be sure about the hidden costs. These can easily mount up, often doubling the cost. Many event organisers will charge you for extra rooms (for workshops or a media launch, for example) or for extra seating or furniture. Check carefully to see what you will be provided with, and be sure that it's OK for you to bring in your own seating or equipment if you wish.

When you discuss prices with an event organiser, they will probably quote you a cost per square foot or metre. What you are quoted is not a price tag, so always negotiate downwards. The organisers will have a target yield per square foot to aim for, so even if there is no scope for a reduction, there are other ways of getting a more favourable deal. Use trade-offs to get a better bargain; for example, agree to pay the full price but insist on free lighting, free tickets and a more prominent entry in the catalogue. Be clear about what you can offer in exchange for a reduction and how you can work together to reach a deal. Remember that as a potential purchaser, you are in a strong position to drive a hard bargain.

Often you are given a certain number of free tickets (if there is a charge to the exhibition) but it could still work out quite expensive if you need all your staff to attend, and you are having to pay their way. And talking of staff, remember that when calculating the cost of your exhibition, you should include staff time in setting up the display and attending the exhibition, as well as accommodation and travel if the event is away from home.

Your budget may look something like this:

EXPENDITURE

Design and photos for exhibition boards	£	2,000
Give-aways – pens and balloons	£	100
Coffee and cups hire	£	100
Staff time (2 staff for 7 hours)	£	140
Stand fees	£	100
TOTAL	£	2,440

ESTIMATED INCOME

Sale of research reports: 55 reports x £2.50	£	137.50
New memberships: 25 memberships x £10	£	250
New memberships: 20 corporate x £30	£	600
Collection on stand	£	25
Sale of mugs: 25 x £1.50	£	37.50
Orders for training manuals: 10 x £100	£	1,000
TOTAL	£	2,050

You might decide on the basis of the above figures that while you will make a 'paper' loss, you still wish to exhibit because:

- you will be reaching an important and influential audience and making useful contacts

- the biggest item, the exhibition boards, will last you many years and will be used time and again

- the photographs commissioned for the boards will be used in your annual report, thus spreading the cost

- it will look bad if you do not exhibit, with 'competitors' wondering why you are not there

MAKING THE MOST OF THE EVENT

To get the best out of an exhibition, you need to put a lot in. That means plenty of homework before the big day. Visit the venue beforehand, and ask someone to show you what the flow of people will be – where they will come in, which way they will head, where the seating and refreshment areas will be, where they will leave by and so on. On the basis of this information, make a decision on the best site for your stand. Contrary to popular belief, the best position is not the stand nearest the entrance, but the second nearest. People are still busy looking at their programme or putting their ticket away immediately they get through the door! If you don't take the trouble to visit the venue, you may end up with a stand in a backwater.

The event organiser will help promote the exhibition, but you should also take some responsibility for marketing it, if only so that you make the very best use of the opportunity. Make sure that people inside and outside your organisation know that you are exhibiting, when and where. Use the exhibition as a chance to write to supporters telling them about it, and inviting them along to take a look. Invite potential corporate donors along, entertain them, display yourself to them in a professional light and show them that you are part of something much bigger. Issue a news release to you local and trade press. Publicise the exhibition in your newsletter. The exhibition itself will offer you opportunities to promote yourself, but don't overlook the other possibilities it offers too.

While you may be exhibiting at an exhibition, there's nothing to stop you from joining in too. Visit other stands, attend workshops and talks, network and promote your organisation to other stallholders.

WHAT ELSE?

Some event organisers run a technical day for exhibitors, some time in advance of the event. It covers the practicalities, such as which loading bay to use, what you can stick on your exhibition shell and what adhesive you can use, how much time you have to set up and take down your stand, and when this is to be done. If yours does not offer such a day, make up a list of questions on practical points such as these and make sure that you get them answered.

If you have anything valuable on your stand, or you are selling things, check the security arrangements, particularly if you have to leave the stand set up overnight. Also check insurance liability (your goods may not be insured once they are off your premises, so you need to check that they are covered by the organiser's insurance, or to make alternative arrangements if necessary).

And finally, always hold a post-mortem. Check your achievements against your objectives to evaluate how successful the venture was. List anything that was particularly good, or that worked especially well. Do the same for the things that were not so good. Learn from your mistakes, and learn from others too. List ideas you picked up from other exhibitors and see if you can use any of them in the future.

CHAPTER ELEVEN

VIDEOS

Video can be a powerful tool, providing it's done well. Home-made efforts with a camcorder will not get you noticed (except, perhaps, on Jeremy Beadle's 'You've Been Framed'!) but a well thought-out and professionally produced video can be a terrific way of getting your message across. It is expensive, though there are ways of doing it for less. Read on to find out what's involved.

If you think that making a video involves little more than picking up a video camera and pointing it, think again. It takes months of work, costs hundreds – though far more likely, thousands – of pounds, and its production will probably cause major disruption in your organisation. And if that's made you think twice, good!

Given that video is probably the most expensive medium you are likely to use, stop and ask if there is a cheaper, easier or more effective way of getting your message across. If there is, use it. However, there is a place for video in the world of charities and voluntary organisations, and many are already using video very successfully:

■ as a promotional tool

■ as a campaigning tool

■ as an information tool

■ as an educational tool

The advantages of video are:

■ it's an excellent way of showing life and situations as they are, in a way that a static picture or words alone could not

■ it's very accessible for people who do not read very well

■ it requires less effort for the audience than a report would

■ it can be a shared experience for the audience

■ a well-produced video can use music, voice-overs, graphics and moving pictures to create a powerful and motivating picture (you only have to think of the effect of that legendary programme, Cathy Come Home, to see the potential)

Another advantage is the versatility of video. Currently, charities are using videos:

- in their reception/foyer, to promote their work to a captive audience of people waiting to be seen

- as a promotional tool at conferences

- in place of, or to back up, speakers at meetings

- to lend to other organisations in order to spread the word

- to sell in order to make money for their work

The disadvantages of video are:

- the cost (not just of the production, but the many extras such as duplication, packaging etc. – see below)

- the time involved

- the disruption to the organisation during filming

- the damage to reputation that can be caused if you do a bad/ unprofessional job

Once you are sure that video is the right medium for you, your next decision is whether to opt for a DIY video or a professionally produced job, though generally your budget will decide this for you.

DIY VIDEOS

Making a video yourself is very time-consuming but great fun if you have the time, energy and help available. Doing it yourself can be an option if you live in a large town or city with a video access centre or community video resource. For a small fee you can get training and the loan of professional equipment, though it's likely that the end product, while being a great deal cheaper than a professionally produced video, will look home-made. Remember that in these days of mass media, people expect very high standards, the same standards, in fact, that they get daily on television. If your efforts are amateurish, people may think that you organisation is also.

To find out about what's available near you, your first ports of call should be the community education department of your local council and your Council for Voluntary Service. Between them they should be able to come up with some good leads.

With camcorders coming down in price, it is possible to make your own video this way, though it takes considerable skill to do it well. Video diaries are increasingly being used on TV, and this has encouraged many people to make their own videos without fully appreciating that clips used on TV are inserted into professionally produced programmes and therefore look far more slick than if you produced one that was entirely filmed on a camcorder with no professional editing. You should not rule out using a camcorder, though you should think carefully about the image you will wish to create and ask whether this will produce it.

Another option is to see if you can persuade a local college with equipment to get the students to make a video for you, as a project. It is likely that colleges will receive many such requests, so take the time to put together a persuasive case on why they should accept your request over some other worthy cause.

USING THE PROFESSIONALS

This option is undoubtedly expensive, setting you back anything from £600 for a very low budget production to around £4,000 for a professional job using a small production company. For this you will get an S-VHS format (see below).

The next step up is Betacam format (see below) which will cost you more still, anything from £4,000 upwards, with £8,000 being the going rate for a 20 minute promotional video.

Talking Technical

Videos are made in different formats. VHS (which stands for Video Home System) is the standard domestic format; our own video recorders are VHS. Domestic camcorders and their smaller sisters, the palmcorders, take VHS and 8mm tape respectively. If you make a video on VHS or 8mm it will lose so much quality during copying and editing that it will be unsuitable for showing; the image will be fuzzy and grainy.

The next notch up is S-VHS (or super VHS), providing better quality, but not as good at the format used by broadcasters – Betacam or its equivalent. If you can afford it, go for the better quality offered by Betacam, though remember that S-VHS will still give you acceptable quality, unlike VHS.

Whatever format is used to make your video, the end result will be copied ('dumped down') onto VHS tape for use in a domestic video recorder. So remember that just because a tape is played on VHS, it does not mean it was made on VHS equipment. The multi-million dollar Hollywood blockbuster you hire from the local video shop will be played on your VHS recorder, but it was made on top quality film.

When you are talking to production companies you may find that practically every sentence a technician utters is peppered with jargon. If you don't understand what they are saying, tell them. If they can't explain it in plain English, find someone who can.

Choosing a Production Company

Going on recommendation is always a good bet, though do talk to more than one company. You should be looking for one that is affordable, professional, and with a good feel for the work that you do, or a sympathetic attitude to it. Always arrange a meeting, never just book a company over the phone. Ask to see a show reel (rather like a moving CV, a showreel is a compilation of their work, to show you what they are capable of). Don't rely on the showreel alone, though, as this will contain only the highlights. Ask to see one or two complete videos too.

You can find video production companies in the Yellow Pages, though the ones listed there are likely to major in corporate work or weddings. A few local authorities produce a screen industry directory, which will list other production companies and associated services (such as companies specialising in duplication – making copies of your video). There's also an organisation called the IVCA, which is the video industry's trade association. They produce some useful background information on producing a video and may be worth a call. Contact IVCA on 0171 580 0962.

When approaching a company, don't tell them your budget, get them to do a costing for you. Revealing that you have £6,000 to spend might mean their fixing a £5,000 video to fit a £6,000 budget.

Costings should be broken down into the three stages of making a video:

Pre-production: this involves research; preparing a story outline (or synopsis); story boarding (a running order and detailed plan of what shots are to be filmed, where and how); scripting

Production: this is the actual filming

Post-Production: this term covers everything that happens after filming, such as off-line editing (rough editing using cheaper equipment) and the next stage, on-line editing (the final editing, carried out on top quality equipment); adding graphics, sound and voice-overs, credits and titles etc.

Setting a Realistic Budget

When you get a quote for a video, it will probably just cover the production. The chances are that there will be many extras you will need to find the money for, over and above your budget for the filming and editing. It is as well that you are aware of these from the start so that you don't run out of money for unexpected additional items. Be sure to include in your budget:

Music – if you are intending to have music of some sort, you have three choices: commission an original score (which is expensive); pay the necessary copyright and seek the necessary permission to use someone else's music (this too is costly) or use a copyright-free recording. Copyright-free music tends to be rather musacky and tacky, but it is an option if you are on a low budget. Your production company can advise you on copyright, commissioning etc. (Never risk using music without the necessary permission: if you are caught, you will be heavily fined and your video will be grounded.)

Packaging – the cover design on the video case will probably not be included as part of the fee, so you will need to budget separately for it.

A celebrity – the price you are quoted should include the cost of a voice-over, but if you want to use a celebrity, you'll need to add extra (unless they are donating their time free, which has been known). See below for advice on this.

Subtitles and signing – (see page 151)

Duplication – you will want more than one copy of your video, and each extra will cost you anything between £6 and £10. Your production company can arrange this for you, though you may find it cheaper to arrange your own duplication by ringing around.

Booklets/leaflets – if you intend to produce a booklet to support the video, or a promotional leaflet, build this into your costs.

Contingency – what happens if one of your key interviewees falls ill on the day of the shoot, or your essential outdoor shot is rained off? You'll need to build in a contingency of 8-10% just in case.

The launch – you will hopefully be so pleased with the end result that you will want to launch it or have a première screening. Allow for the cost of this too.

Clinching the Deal

Once you have decided who is going to make your video, make sure you read any contract they issue you with very carefully. It may contain clauses you are unhappy about. Agree in writing what the budget price includes and what it doesn't. When you accept a quote for video production, your acceptance letter should stipulate that any additional costs must be agreed in writing before go-ahead. Payment terms also need to be spelt out (for example, half the fees payable on completion of filming and the balance on delivery of the video).

Build into the contract a penalty for delays. This is particularly important if you need the video in time for a particular event. Find out about arrangements your production company has in place to avoid delays caused by staff being sick or equipment being stolen. And on the subject of theft, check that you are not responsible if their equipment is stolen or damaged on location.

COPYRIGHT

You need to make sure that you are the copyright holder of the video, so get this in writing when you agree a contract. If you don't, copyright will remain with the production company. They will also retain copyright to all footage (known as 'rushes') shot for, though not necessarily used in, your film, so ensure you get this copyright too, or you might find your material popping up in someone else's video.

CELEBRITIES

If you use the right celebrity you can turn a pedestrian video into one with a bit a pazazz, and it needn't cost the earth. The Charity Commission has produced a video on the responsibilities of trustees. It could have been a bit dull and dry, but Lenny Henry brings it to life. Apart from being very funny, his link with Comic Relief makes him a suitable celebrity for a video aimed at charity people.

Picking a suitable celebrity (and one you can afford) is essential. A video on benefits aimed at a Scottish audience could do worse than book Billy Connolly. He's down-to-earth, straight-speaking, funny, and a Scot. A Blue Peter presenter would not really fit the bill in the same way! So when picking a celebrity, think about your audience and what will appeal to them.

Using a celebrity at the going rate can work out quite expensive, though you can often persuade them to do it for free if you are a cause dear to their heart and the task is not too onerous. If you are paying a famous face for their trouble, you might find that they will want a larger fee if the video is being sold rather than given away, so check this one carefully at the outset. Always get a contract so that your celebrity can't suddenly pull out, as has been known.

CONSENT

It's a good idea to get consent, preferably in writing, from anyone who is going to appear in your video. It has been known for people to come back at a later date arguing that they didn't know what you were planning to do with the film, or that you misled them. The consent form should outline what the footage is being used for, so that you are fully covered.

SUBTITLES, SIGNING AND TRANSLATION

You might decide to make your video as accessible as possible by adding subtitles and/or a signer (for deaf viewers), or by doing foreign language voice-overs for people who do not understand English. This will add significantly to your costs, because you will need to employ a translator, editor and someone to do the dubbing or signing. It's all highly skilled work, and it will lengthen your production timescale.

LENGTH

Most organisations start off with a 30 minute video in mind, perhaps because this is the length of many TV programmes. It is not, however, the length of most videos, which are between five and 15 minutes. Deciding how you are going to use the video will help you settle the length, so a video for your reception should be very brief, as people will pass through fairly quickly. A video to support a speaker at a meeting will need to be short enough to allow a talk and discussion afterwards, while a video designed to replace a speaker altogether will need to be longer.

> **TIP**
> If your video is receiving funding – from your local authority, for example – do let them see a copy of the script well before the final video is put together. If you don't, you could find that they insist on the film being grounded if they have a major disagreement with something you've said.

If you are bringing in the professionals, it's a good idea to assign someone to accompany them on filming days. One of your staff will have a better idea of the kinds of images you are looking for and those best avoided, and will be on hand to provide guidance, check that everything is going smoothly, and to sort out any problems.

VIDEO CHECKLIST

Still thinking of making a video? Then work through the following questions, which will help you decide whether to go ahead, and will form the basis of a brief if you intend to use a production company:

■ Why do you want to make a video?

■ Is there another way of achieving the same objectives just as effectively?

■ How will you use the video? Where will you show it? (e.g. at public meetings/in the foyer/for staff induction)

■ Who will it be aimed at? What audience?

■ What will it be about? What issues will you cover? (list those that must be covered and those you would like covered if it is possible within the time)

■ Where will it be filmed? How many locations?

■ When do you want it ready? (It will take at least four months, and probably nearer six, from start of project to finish – assuming everything goes according to plan. Double that timescale if you are doing it yourself and require training before you begin)

■ How long will it last?

■ Do you need a celebrity? If so, why? Who?

■ Will you require graphics? What sort (tables, charts etc.)?

LAUNCHING YOUR VIDEO

After all the work that you put into making a video, the least you can do is to launch it. Book a small cinema if appropriate (try to persuade the owner to let you use it at cost) and organise a première for your staff, supporters, funders and those you are seeking to influence. Turn the occasion into an event, and get the local or specialist media along too if you can.

Promote the video (if it is for sale or hire) by issuing a news release to relevant publications, supported by a still photo from the filming. Be ready with supplies to send out in response to enquiries you are bound to get. Keep a list of those who enquire, buy or hire, and do a follow-up letter to them in a few months' time to ask them to support your cause (if they don't already).

VIDEO BRIEF

Client: **One World Third World**

Video: **Food For All, Poverty For None**

Background to One World Third World

We are a British-based charity dedicated to raising money for development and educational projects in the third world and to raising awareness of the causes of underdevelopment.

Reason for the video

We require a video to assist our fundraisers at public meetings by providing them with audio-visual material to back-up their presentations.

Audience

Church groups, women's groups, student groups and secondary schools.

Where will it be shown?

In church and school halls on domestic video equipment.

Messages

- Third world hunger and poverty is curable, but aid alone will not achieve it: economic change is required too.
- People in this country have a role to play in fundraising to support educational and employment projects abroad.
- Boycotting goods from oppressive third world regimes and buying goods from countries with good human rights records will help stimulate local economies and act as a lever to oppressive governments.

Communication of the message

This will take the form of library pictures of third world poverty mixed with interviews with experts in this country. There will also be scenes of people in Britain supporting the third world by buying the right supermarket products and by fundraising.

Locations

Two interviews with experts at two different London locations
One interview in Bristol
Footage of people buying products at the supermarket and One World shop
Footage of our fundraisers in action

Graphics

1 map and 5 bar charts, one caricature cartoon

Required audience response

- a better understanding of the causes of third world poverty
- a belief that they can do something to help
- a commitment to action by changing their buying behaviour and by donating to a development project

Length

As it will be used in addition to a speaker, it must not exceed 10 minutes

Required by

Our next fundraising drive begins in September next year, so the videos would be required no later than mid-August.

CHAPTER TWELVE

ADVERTISING AND SPONSORSHIP

The world of advertising has a glamorous, flash image which stands uncomfortably alongside the more down-to-earth work of the voluntary sector. But advertising is a powerful tool, and many of the larger charities are making increasing use of it to achieve a number of worthwhile objectives. Charities feel more comfortable using sponsorship, although many are very poor at attracting it. This chapter shows you how you can use advertising effectively and how to become better at gaining sponsorship from companies.

Look through the colour supplements or your daily newspaper to see sophisticated adverts from some of Britain's leading charities. Just as Coca Cola, ICI and other multi-nationals make use of advertising because it works, so too do charities.

It's obvious why companies advertise: they have a product or service that they need to sell in order to remain in business, and they all have competitors in the same boat. But why do charities need to advertise? Some do so to attract donations, others to raise awareness of an issue. But what about the many charities which are service-providers? It's likely that their 'product' is so much in demand that it outstrips supply! Surely there is no need to attract even more users than can be dealt with?

For all charities, including those which provide a service, there is a need to ensure that their work is recognised and valued, so that they can attract funding – from corporate supporters, local and national government, and the public. Public relations can help achieve this, and so can advertising. It's not appropriate for all charities, but it might be right for you.

By advertising, you can promote your work and get public support for it, as well as bringing your achievements to the attention of decision-makers and potential partners. You need not advertise your services: you can simply promote your philosophy and approach. (There will, of course, for some organisations, be times when you wish to promote the services you offer.)

WHAT IS THE DIFFERENCE BETWEEN ADVERTISING AND PUBLIC RELATIONS?

Although both are aspects of marketing, public relations and advertising are not the same. The crucial difference is that editorial coverage secured by PR is not paid for, while advertising media coverage is – and can be extremely costly.

The advantage of advertising over PR is that it is much more precise. As advertiser, you decide what you want to say, who you want to say it to, and when you want to say it. You define the message via the advert's words and visuals, target the audience by selecting the right publication, and choose the exact timing. Unlike PR, your coverage is guaranteed; it is not left to chance.

The drawback is that this kind of flexibility costs money. A less obvious disadvantage is that editorial coverage is regarded as impartial, and therefore carries more weight than advertising, which is known to be paid for. Ideally, advertising and PR methods should be used in conjunction.

HOW TO WRITE AN EFFECTIVE AND PERSUASIVE ADVERTISEMENT

Just as writing a publicity leaflet is an art, so too is producing effective advertising copy. That's why there are so many advertising agencies, and so many big companies with huge budgets to spend. Chances are you will never develop the skills of a professional advertising copywriter (though if you do, you might want to consider a lucrative career change!) but you probably can improve the work you currently produce.

Good advertising should follow the **AIDA** formula:

- it should attract **ATTENTION** so that people stop to read it. You can use a strong photograph or other image, a headline, bold colours, striking design, or a combination of these to achieve this.

- it must attract the reader's **INTEREST** so that they will read on and develop an interest in your work or in the issue you are trying to promote.

- it should stimulate **DESIRE** – to work with you, to work for you, to use your facilities, to fund you, to campaign for your cause, to support you.

- it must prompt **ACTION** – to encourage potential partners to get in touch, to persuade potential sponsors to get their chequebooks out, to get supporters writing letters to their MPs in support of your campaign.

If your advertisement is aimed at attracting donations, you should try to put a price on what you do, to give donors a real idea of how their cash will be spent. For example, instead of simply asking for money, why not say "£5 will buy this child her sight" or "Your £1 will save a seafish". Both these statements would work well as attention-grabbing headlines, and, combined with a photograph, could create powerful advertising.

Try to keep your copy to a minimum, and your request as simple as possible. Complex advertisements do not work, because readers simply do not have the time, and often cannot spare the effort, to wade through your advert or to sort out the messages.

Consider using a coupon response. This makes it really easy for readers to send in for further information or to mail you a donation. If you are using this device, remember to put your address on the coupon rather than in the body of the advertisement; if a reader loses the advert having cut off the coupon, they will still know where to send it.

> **TIP**
>
> *Combining a freepost address (if you can afford to – contact Royal Mail for prices) can also make it easier for readers to respond. So can a freephone number. British Telecom and Mercury both offer this service via their 0800 and 0500 numbers.*

If you are using coupons in different publications, code the coupon so you can tell where it was cut out from. This will enable you to monitor response to your advert, and to assess which publication produced the best response, invaluable if you are planning to advertise again.

Adverts designed to generate sales should adopt a different approach. You need to decide whether you want to promote the product itself, or concentrate on explaining to readers how you will spend the profit made from the sale of the product. In other words, do you want to say "Top quality silk blouse with hand embroidered motif, available in a range of fashionable colours" or "Buy one of our quality silk blouses and help sick children at an orphanage in Delhi"?

A slogan is always useful in your adverts. You can probably think of scores of commercial slogans, such as "Reaches the parts other beers can't reach" or "Guinness is good for you". They are not terribly clever, but they have caught on. Try to come up with a slogan for your organisation that is both appropriate to what you do, and at the same time clever – through its use of puns, alliteration or careful balance.

To take another example from the commercial world, a leading discount supermarket chain came up with "*Underspend* your budget, *overspill* your trolley." This slogan works through its use of two words, "underspend" and "overspill," which balance wonderfully. Other examples include "The *little* car with *big* ideas" and "*High* on taste, *low* on fat". Try this technique for yourself.

LOCAL NEWSPAPERS

Advantages: By using local newspapers you can target your message to a particular geographical area. The newspaper will often help you to design the advert for free, although don't expect anything too sophisticated. You can act quickly – there's no long lead-in time.

Disadvantages: Particularly in free newspapers, your advert has to compete for attention against many others. Reproduction is often poor. Newspapers have a very short shelf life.

NATIONAL NEWSPAPERS

Advantages: National papers are read by decision-makers and professionals, so it is a good way of reaching these audiences. There are fewer adverts to compete with than in local papers. You can act quickly – there's no long lead-in time.

Disadvantages: Geographical targeting is poorer than for local papers, so there is considerable wastage. It is much more expensive than advertising in local papers. Reproduction can be poor. Daily newspapers have an even shorter shelf life than weekly freesheets.

PROFESSIONAL/TRADE MAGAZINES

Advantages: Targeting your audience is easier – if you want to reach health professionals, you are more likely to do so with an advert in Health Service Journal than in the Motherwell Mercury! There is generally better reproduction and fewer adverts to compete with. The shelf life is longer.

Disadvantages: It is more expensive, with longer lead-in times.

HOW TO WRITE AN INTERESTING ADVERTORIAL

An advertorial is an advertising feature, but it is designed so that it does not look like an advertisement – it is presented to look like editorial and comprises an article or feature rather than a traditional advert. Its name comes from combining 'advert' and 'editorial'. It is paid for, and in return for your cash, you get to say what you want to about yourself – within limits – unlike in a genuine editorial feature.

Advertorials used to be limited to free papers and the more downmarket trade publications, but they are being used more now by the qualities, especially some of the Sunday colour supplements, and have become an important source of revenue for newspaper and magazine publishers. According to research commissioned by PR Week, the number of advertorial pages increased overall by 47% between 1991 and 1992. In the quality press they went from four pages in 1991 to 19 in 1992. For the mid-market press the figures rose from 16 to 73, and for the popular press the increase was from nothing to 45.

It is extremely unlikely that you would ever place an advertorial in the Sunday papers; it would leave you very definitely in the red – an advertorial in The Sunday Times colour supplement or in a popular lifestyle magazine could set you back tens of thousands of pounds! So on the whole, you will be dealing with specialist publications and free papers.

Advertorial policy varies according to the publication. Some will get one of their reporters to interview you about your work, and then to write a feature. Others will ask you to supply the copy. This is a better opportunity, because you can say exactly what you wish, but it can be hard work. Where do you start? What should you say? How can you find a story angle?

> **TIP**
>
> *If you decide to place an advert in a trade publication, ask them if you can have some editorial too. Although few publications will admit to their magazine being advertising-led, in practice you can often secure editorial by placing an advert. It's always worth a try.*

If you produce good copy, the benefits will outweigh the effort involved, but if you put together a boring feature, no one will read it and you will have wasted your money. Journalists train for years, so do not expect to be able to churn out a story the way they do. Writing is definitely an art, but by giving consideration to the following points before you set pen to paper, you should find the task easier and the end result better. You might also find it useful to refer to the section on copywriting in Chapter Five.

- Find out from the publication how many words they are looking for – it's easier to write to a target figure than to try to edit later on.

- Make sure you are familiar with the publication and its style – try to use the same style when writing your copy.

- Get a story angle. You need a theme or line – preferably something unusual. What makes you or your service different? Are you doing anything innovative or pioneering? Do you offer a special approach?

- The first paragraph is crucial – if you fail to capture the reader's attention here, they are unlikely to read on. Don't save your best line for the end – the reader might never get that far. Lead with it!

- Don't forget about headlines – your headline might be rewritten by the publication, but try to think of one anyway, as they will not rewrite a good and apt headline, and if you leave it to the newspaper or magazine, they might get it wrong.

- Use short sub-headings to help you break up the text into readable chunks and to link different themes.

■ Before you begin to write, jot down the key points that you want to get across in your article. Tick them off your list as you write about them.

■ If you are writing for a free newspaper, remember to emphasise local connections, even if you operate nationally. If you are writing for an Plymouth paper, readers will not be interested in your services or offices in Aberdeen!

■ Think about your audience – are they professionals who will understand the terms you are using, or are you writing for people who will be unfamiliar with your particular terminology? Use appropriate language.

■ Use case histories to bring your feature to life, with lots of real-life examples of how your charity has helped change lives. If you are concerned about the confidentiality of your clients or service-users, change names and other details.

■ Try to make your advertorial appear independent. Quote people from other organisations and use facts and figures to support your case.

> **TIP**
>
> *To improve the appearance of your advertorial, supply a range of good quality photographs and illustrations. Make sure they are suitably captioned – if you don't, the publication will caption them in a bland way, or might even get the captions wrong. You can ask for the return of your photos, but don't send anything very prized if it is your only copy, as pictures do have a tendency to get lost.*

Some publications make extra money by charging advertisers an exorbitant additional fee for colour separation. This is a necessary technical process involving separating your colour photos into cyan, yellow, magenta and black, the four printing colours. If you are asked to supply photographs, enquire if there is an extra charge for colour separation, and if there is, you might find it a great deal cheaper to opt for black and white photographs instead, or to get your pictures colour separated elsewhere.

There is some debate about the ethics of advertorials, and you should be aware of this if you are considering using one. Some people feel that advertorials, in trying to pass themselves off as editorial, are tricking the reader. (The Periodical Publishers' Association produces guidelines on the labelling of advertorials.) Then there's the contrary view that they are a waste of money simply because everyone knows that they are paid for and so they're not read. There are journalists who feel that they erode a publication's credibility and bring their profession into disrepute, because advertorials are clearly not independent articles.

But what do the readers think? A survey carried out by National Opinion Polls in 1993 revealed that the majority of readers can distinguish among advertisements, advertorials and editorials. Alarmingly, however, 46% of respondents said that the information in advertorials was as convincing as information in editorials, and 8% said that it was more convincing! So perhaps advertorials do pull the wool over readers' eyes.

OTHER ADVERTISING OPPORTUNITIES

When we think of advertising, we tend to have in mind newspapers and trade magazines – television advertising is out of the question for most charities. But there are alternatives worth considering. Here's an Alphabetical Guide to Advertising Opportunities:

■ **A sign outside your office** – never overlook the obvious. A sign outside your office, setting out what you do, is an excellent way of reaching people with your message. Check on whether you require planning permission, though.

■ **Bill boards** – these used to be used only by companies advertising products. Political parties then cottoned to their use, and now pressure groups and charities are making successful use of them. It's not cheap, but it certainly has impact.

■ **Buses** – advertising inside the bus and on the back of it can be excellent value, a great deal cheaper than bus shelter advertising. With some bus companies you can also advertise on the back of bus tickets. If you want to attract motorists, opt for back-of-the-bus advertising. Obviously bus ticket and bus interior advertising tends to reach lower socio-economic groups and women with children (except in London). These might be your audience (if you are advertising a service) while if you want donations, you might get more success using back-of-the-bus ads to reach more affluent motorists.

■ **Cinema** – cinema advertising can be really tacky, so be careful, but if you can produce a good advert, it could be an excellent way of reaching the right audience.

■ **Conference programmes** – if you are exhibiting at a conference, you might wish to place an advert in the conference programme. Don't forget other programmes, too, such as theatre programmes, which are a good way of reaching decision-makers.

■ **Direct mail** – this is jargon for writing to people you don't know! Don't underestimate the value of direct mail as a cost-effective way of targeting audiences, if done properly. If targeting is not good, it's a great way of wasting money, as you will know from the amount of junk mail you receive through your own front door! You can buy mailing lists, or compile your own, and you can use companies to organise your distribution, or do it yourself.

- **Directories** – most professions produce directories and handbooks, and a listing in one of these can help get you known, though think carefully about whether the readers form part of your target audience

- **Door-to-door** – this method of direct mail is cheap and often used by charities. Quite simply you put leaflets through letterboxes. What could be easier?

- **Eggs** – in 1994, British Telecom became the first UK company to use eggvertising, where messages are blown with high pressure jets onto the outside of fresh eggs. There is scope here, for larger charities, for some original and creative ad campaigns.

- **Flyers and posters** – leaflets and other publications are a good way of advertising your services. Leave them not just in your own reception, but in libraries, community centres and other public places where they are likely to be seen by your target audience.

- **Franking stamps** – if you have a franking machine, why not get your logo and slogan incorporated?

- **LED displays** – some public places such as swimming pools and sports centres offer an advertising service via large LED displays which display your message. It's a cheap and easy way to advertise.

- **Pay and display car parking tickets** – in many towns and cities it is possible to advertise on the back of these.

- **Piggy-backing** – this is direct mail sent as an insert in someone else's mailing. For example, sending a leaflet about your charity in the newsletter of a local voluntary organisation.

- **Posters** – whether you get them properly printed or make your own, you can reach a lot of people with a poster.

- **Post Office franks** – if you don't have your own franking machine, you can still get your message across by getting the post office to frank other people's letters with your logo.

- **Radio** – local independent radio reaches a large audience and is not always expensive to advertise on. Most homes have more than one radio and 95% of all cars have one. Call your local station and have an informal chat with their advertising department about the possibilities and costs.

- **Sandwich boards** – the humble sandwich board is no longer in vogue, but look at old photos of city street scenes and you will see them advertising everything from Horlicks to tailor-made suits. Sandwich boards are easy to make and have novelty value.

> **TIP**
>
> *When you place adverts, make sure your staff – especially your switchboard – know. You are likely to receive calls as a result, and you need to ensure that they are handled professionally. Make sure someone is available to deal with enquiries that result, and that, if necessary, packs or other promotional material, 'thank you' letters and receipts, publications and campaigning materials are ready for sending to people who get in touch.*

- **Taxis** – black cabs now take adverts, both inside and outside the cabs. Contact local firms for details of schemes in your area.

- **Vehicles** – if you supply cars to staff, or have a minibus, use the vehicle as a mobile advertisement. Get it painted in your corporate colours, complete with logo and slogan, if you have one.

- **Yellow Pages** – another obvious one, but also very affordable and effective.

GETTING ADVERTISING FOR FREE

If you have the nerve and the energy, it's possible to get substantial advertising features for free.

Contact a trade newspaper that you know carries advertorials and offer them some quality editorial on one of your projects or services, or on an issue or subject that is likely to interest their readers . Suggest in the covering letter to the editor that other organisations who worked with you on the project (suppliers or corporate donors, for example) might consider advertising if they knew a feature on the project was planned. Enclose a list of your suppliers/partners/donors. The rest is up to the magazine! Ask the magazine to let you know by a particular deadline whether or not they intend to use your article. You can always offer it elsewhere if it is rejected. The benefit of this approach is that the publication may decide to carry your article anyway, even without your suppliers or donors advertising. This sometimes works with local freesheets too.

Remember, though, that the article you send must be interesting, newsy and well-written if it is to stand a chance of being used.

Another way of getting an advert for free is to use the listings column in your local freesheet. Most local freebies have a section or diary where they publicise community events, talks and sales, and usually there is no charge for this if you are not a commercial enterprise. Freesheets often have a help/request column too. You can use this to advertise for volunteers and helpers.

Job Advertisements

One type of advertisement nearly every charity has placed at one time or another is the job advert. Often little thought and consideration go into these, and great opportunities are therefore missed. It is sensible to regard the job ad as dual purpose: it should attract applicants for a particular job *and* it

> **TRUE STORY**
>
> A new take away restaurant placed some expensive adverts in the local papers to publicise its opening and splendid food. It sounded so good that I decided to try it out, but the advert did not include an address or phone number. I was left with a watering mouth, but the restaurateur was left heavily out of pocket.
>
> His mistake was a surprisingly common one. The advert's copy was supplied on headed notepaper, and no one thought to write out the contact details as part of the advert. Perhaps they assumed the newspaper would take care of it or maybe they simply didn't think. Make sure you never make this mistake when advertising.

should promote your organisation to those who are idly scanning the jobs pages.

As with any advert, you should think carefully about the wording in a job advertisement because it will be read by a great many people. Instead of simply passing on information about the position you are advertising, use it to say something about your organisation, your values and your approach.

So instead of saying "Anytown Hospice needs a nurse. 39 hours per week. Salary £..."

Try saying "We're dedicated to giving people the chance to die in dignity, with their friends and family around them. We're looking for a nurse who is as committed as we are to the hospice movement to join our team..."

Anyone reading the latter would have a much clearer idea about the sort of organisation you are, whether they want to apply for your job or not.

TO ADVERTISE OR NOT TO ADVERTISE – THAT IS THE QUESTION!

Advertising is, as we have already said, a powerful tool – but not always! It can help to change attitudes and to reach important audiences, but it can also be a big waste of money if not approached with care and understanding.

It is not unusual for charities to be contacted by the advertising departments of publications about the possibility of their advertising. Before you accept an offer, think carefully and ask yourself and the publication the following questions:

- What would be the purpose of our advertising? What would we hope to achieve?

- What is the circulation of the publication? What is the target audience for this publication? Is this an audience we wish to reach? (The publication's advertising department will have all of this information, so don't hesitate to ask for it.)

- What is the cost? Could we use this money more effectively in another way?

- How is this publication regarded? Is it read and respected or just glanced at and binned by its readers?

- Who else will be advertising? Is there any clash or conflict?

■ What would be involved? Would we have to supply camera-ready artwork? (See page 111) How much would this add to the cost?

■ What would our supporters think? Might they feel that we were wasting their money on "PR" when it should go straight to the user?

Only ever agree to placing an advert when you are confident that you will achieve benefits in doing so. Never advertise just because it seems like a good idea at the time, or because there's a special offer with reduced rates.

Notoriously, insurance policies are *sold* to the public, rather than *bought* by them. Often the same is true of advertising and those who pay for it. Make sure that you are spending money only because you know what you are getting, and that you're sure that it's worth to you what you are paying for it.

Finally, remember that one household name, The Body Shop, has never advertised, but relies for its coverage on PR-generated stories.

MAKING MONEY FROM ADVERTISING AND SPONSORSHIP

So far we have concentrated on charities *spending* money on advertising. You can also *make* money from it.

When you produce an important document, such as your annual report, you might like to investigate off-setting the production costs by getting sponsorship or adverts from your suppliers. Why not get in touch with your bank, accountant, solicitors and others to see if they would like to take out a small advert in your publication? Or for bigger charities, perhaps one of your corporate donors could help by getting it designed or printed using their in-house facilities?

The same goes for newsletters. Smaller, local charities, who do not have corporate donors and the pulling power of the bigger organisations, can make money here, too. There is no reason why you should not approach local bakers, hairdressers, shops and restaurants to get them to buy space.

They will want to know the readership, circulation, frequency of publication and cost, so have all this information ready when you speak to businesses. Why not try some direct mail to reach potential advertisers? A sample mailshot is enclosed for attracting advertising for a tenants' newsletter and for seeking sponsorship for a publication.

Brippington Animal Welfare

27 Main Street, Brippington
Tel. 01998 12345

Timothy Thomson
Timmy's Vegetarian Restaurant
12 High Street
Brippington BR12 8AJ

December 10th

Dear Mr. Thomson,

I would like to tell you about a very special offer we are making – for a limited period only – to local businesses in Brippington.

We are currently putting together our February issue of 'Paws for a Cause', a high quality newsletter which we produce every quarter for our 1,000 supporters in Brippington. We have decided, for the first time ever, to take advertising, and to mark the occasion, we will be offering some special deals which we believe you might be interested in taking advantage of.

For just £100 you can place a quarter page advert in our February issue. If you reserve your space before the end of the year, we will give you a 10% discount voucher to use if you decide to advertise in our May issue. I'm sure you will agree that our rates compare extremely well with the local newspaper, and you will be reaching an audience with a very high proportion of vegetarians among it, many of them living within walking distance of your restaurant.

In addition to some back issues, I have enclosed a rate card, copy deadlines for the next four issues, and further details of some special advertising deals. I will telephone you by the end of next week to see if you are interested in finding out more.

Yours sincerely

Helen Jones
Director

Encl.

Brippington Animal Welfare

27 Main Street, Brippington
Tel. 01998 12345

Megan Griffiths
Managing Director
Brippington Pet Foods
59 High Street
Brippington BR12 8BT

10th December

Dear Megan,

I think I may have mentioned to you when we last met that we are preparing a new promotional leaflet on the work of our charity and are currently seeking sponsorship for its production. There are, we believe, mutual benefits in our organisations working together on this project.

The leaflet will be circulated to animal lovers, animal welfare charities and pet shops across the county, and they in turn will circulate further copies to their own contacts. In total, 5,000 copies of the leaflet will be distributed to animal lovers and animal owners, with the leaflets reaching many of your own targets.

Full credit will be given for your sponsorship in our quarterly newsletter, and we will encourage our members to opt for your pet products over those of your competitors. They are always keen to support companies that offer us support.

I have enclosed a copy of our old promotional leaflet to give you an idea of the sort of thing we have in mind.

We are looking for around £3,000 for overall sponsorship of the leaflet, although we are willing to consider joint sponsorship at a reduced rate if this would suit your budget better. There is also the possibility of help in kind, such as the use of your in-house design team, for example.

I realise that so close to Christmas you must be busy trying to clear your desk, but I will call you next week for an informal chat about this project.

Yours sincerely

Helen Jones
Director

Encl.

PROJECT SPONSORSHIP

Attracting sponsorship for publications is just one aspect of project sponsorship, i.e. getting support for a particular project or promotion (as opposed to general sponsorship of your charity). Getting your organisation sponsored is extremely difficult unless you have a very high profile. Since most charities do not fall into this category, project sponsorship is what you will aim for.

Companies receive letters every week asking for money. Multinationals might receive in their mailbag many thousands each year, and most only get a standard "thank you but no thank you" letter in reply. How can you increase your chances of success?

Start by doing your homework. Only send letters seeking sponsorship to companies likely to consider supporting you, either because they have a known interest in the sort of work you do, they have sponsored you (or a similar charity) in the past, or where there is an obvious link (e.g. Mothercare and a children's charity, The Co-op Bank and a co-operative organisation, a brewer and a project to help alcoholics, an oil company and a wildlife or environmental project or charity).

If your knowledge of companies is not very good, get hold of copies of A Guide to UK Company Giving and Finding Company Sponsors for Local Causes from the Directory of Social Change, 24 Stephenson Way, London NW1 2DP. Another relatively new publication, the Hollis Sponsorship and Donations Yearbook, is also available from your reference library, containing an A-Z of the UK's top sponsoring and donating companies. It lists names and addresses of companies, the name and job title of the person to contact, their sponsorship budgets, details of who they sponsor, and information on their donations policy. It is also used by companies looking for a charity to sponsor, so you might want to consider placing an entry (for a fee).

Next, phone up and get the name of the person to write to (or use the above directory, although remember that people move jobs, and all directories are out of date as soon as they are published). Letters to a named person show that you have done some research; they have a head start over those beginning 'Dear Sir'.

Don't send the same letter to everyone on your list; personalised letters stand a far better chance of success. Use core paragraphs in all the letters, if you wish, but always add a personal touch which shows that you know something about the organisation you are writing to.

Keep your letter brief, but enclose background information. Make the letter as persuasive as possible by spelling out clearly:

■ what's in it for the company – what they would get out of it – how it would enhance their image

- how it could help them with their business objectives

- why they should do it – what the link is with your charity

- what audience they would be reaching in sponsoring your project or campaign

- how cost-effective it is

In the background briefing notes include:

- a full description of the project you are seeking sponsorship for, including the project's objectives

- details of what the project involves (e.g. a newsletter, press advertising campaign, new premises, posters, a worker...)

- a clear breakdown of all costs (not just those you want help with)

- a list of other supporters (if it is an exclusive sponsorship that you have on offer, say so and 'sell' it as a plus)

- how much money you would like from that potential supporter and what it would be spent on

- how they would get acknowledgement (e.g. a mention in all of your news releases, their logo on your leaflet, an article in your newsletter....)

> **TIP**
>
> *Timing is important. If you make an approach for a small sum of money towards the end of the financial year, you might hit lucky. Companies are busy trying to use up their budgets and may therefore be more responsive to approaches at this time. If you are seeking a larger sum, this is the wrong time to get in touch, as the budget might be nearly exhausted and unable to accommodate a large sponsorship request.*

Setting up sponsorship can take many months or even years, so start early. And be prepared for a lot of rejections. Attracting sponsorship is hard work, it is very competitive, and you will get many knock-backs, but don't lose heart or give up. If you have a good project, with company appeal, you will get support sooner or later. Just look at the thousands of charities which do get support every year.

THE COST OF ADVERTISING

The price of placing an advert varies a great deal, according to demand as well as other factors, such as:

- the bigger the advert, the more expensive it will be – a half page will cost more than a quarter page, though not necessarily twice as much

- the bigger the circulation of a publication, the more you will have to pay for your space

- the situation of your advertisement will also affect price – a front page advert is more expensive than one on an inside page

- colour is more expensive than black and white, both to produce artwork for and to print

TIP

If you are planning to place a series of adverts in the same publication, you can generally negotiate a discount.

FINDING OUT ABOUT COST

Advertising departments produce 'rate cards'. These set out the cost of adverts, according to size, position and so on. Often the rate printed on the rate card is open to negotiation, so always try to get the official rate reduced if you can.

Like other things, advertising costs vary a great deal, and are subject to inflation. For this reason, we have not set out rates here, but if you want guidelines on current rates, go to your public library, where you can consult a monthly publication, British Rate and Data (BRAD), which lists all the UK's advertising media, their rates and their readership.

If appropriate, you might consider teaming up with another charity, or a group of organisations in your area, to place an advert. This will spread the cost and promote a united front.

Once you have placed an advert, it's likely that you will get a range of enquiries, by phone and by mail. Make sure that your receptionist knows what to do when someone calls in response to an advert. Some callers may wish to speak to someone, in addition to receiving an information pack. Make sure a knowledgeable member of staff is available.

You will need to ensure that you have prepared packs ready to send out to enquirers. You might wish to include in the packs:

■ a covering letter thanking the enquirer for getting in touch (if you have the resources, put the core letter on a word processor and run off personalised versions, with the enquirer's name and address, the current date, and an introductory paragraph that is relevant to their enquiry)

■ a copy of your annual report

■ any other information about your organisation

Who is likely to contact you following an ad promotion? This all depends on where you placed your advertisement. For adverts in your local paper, the chances are that you will get a fair amount of interest from local people who would like to support you or use your services. You might also get enquiries from schoolchildren doing projects, from schoolteachers looking for general information, and from students. You might need to produce three or four standard letters of response.

For adverts placed in trade and professional publications, fewer enquiries are likely to result, and they are more likely to be from those with a professional interest. Because trade publications tend to have a longer shelf-life than local papers, you should expect enquiries to continue to arrive in dribs and drabs for some months.

Monitoring interest

When you place an advertisement, keep a log of enquiries. That way you can build up a picture of the best places to advertise, taking into account audience and cost.

HAVE A GO YOURSELF

Have a go at making the following advertisement more likely to attract both interest and donations.

THE DEVINGVILLE CATS' PROTECTION SQUAD

The Devingville Cats' Protection Squad was set up by Mrs. Gladys Arthur OBE, who generously left the charity £100,000 of her estate, which has been used to upgrade the cattery facilities. The Squad has been in existence for over 40 years. In that time it has helped over 50,000 cats. The Squad now help around 2,000 cats in Devingville every year, providing them with a comfy kennel and two meals per day.

All of this costs money, and can only be continued with the support of donors. So please open your chequebook today and send a donation. Cheques made payable to Devingville Cats' Protection Squad should be sent to PO Box 3, Devingville DV11 9AB.

DISCUSSION

This advertisement makes some common though elementary mistakes:

■ Its headline is not designed to attract attention and encourage the reader to read on

■ It contains too much irrelevant background information and facts and figures

■ It fails to exploit the reader's interest in cats by throwing in an emotive appeal

■ The copy is dull

□ □ □ □ □ □ □ □ □ □ □ □ □ □

IT'S A DOG'S LIFE BEING A CAT IN DEVINGVILLE!
Help an abandoned moggy for the price of a Kit Kat

You can help an injured or abandoned cat for just 35p. That's what it costs a day to keep a moggy at the Devingville Cats' Protection Squad. Over the last 40 years we have helped tens of thousands of cats in desperate need and now it's your turn to help us.

We need £10,000 to enable us to stay open this year. If everyone in Devingville were to forgo just one bar of chocolate this year, and give the money to us instead, it would enable us to remain open and to expand our services. How many bars of chocolate are you willing to give up to help cats?

I am going to give up some chocolate to help Devingville's cats. I enclose:

❏ £1   ❏ £5   ❏ £10   ❏ £15   ❏ Other £_____

Cheques made payable to Devingville Cats' Protection Squad should be sent to PO Box 3, Devingville DV11 9AB.

DISCUSSION

This is much better:

- ■ The headline attracts attention and is intriguing
- ■ It is written in the first person, which gives it more appeal
- ■ It appeals to the reader direct
- ■ It quantifies what help means (a bar of chocolate)
- ■ it has a coupon response to make replying easier
- ■ The copy hints that closure might result if people do not help, although it does not say this explicitly
- ■ It cuts out unnecessary background material and detail
- ■ It uses emotive words, such as 'injured' and 'abandoned', which are designed to appeal to cat-lovers

CUSTOMER CARE

Companies such as Marks and Spencer and Kwik Fit are famous for their customer care. British Rail and British Telecom, once noted for their distinct lack of it, have pulled up their socks and are receiving praise from unlikely sources for their efforts. Thanks to various charter initiatives, even the public sector is improving its customer care and developing more of a client focus. If you want to be better at customer care, or if it's something you have never given much thought to, then read on.

What has customer care got to do with voluntary organisations, who by their nature are non profit-making, with no customers? Well, there is a great deal that you can learn from business, with its commercial attitude to customer care. Combined with your principled stance and caring outlook, it will make yours an altogether better organisation.

Some charities, those which run shops, for example, clearly have customers: there are over 8,000 charity shops in Britain. But many voluntary organisations feel that customer care is only relevant to those charities with shops; it is not something that concerns them. Yet all organisations deal with 'customers' of sorts. You might sell the publications you produce, or perhaps you run training courses. The people buying your briefing papers or attending your courses are customers and you need to take good care of them.

WHO ARE YOUR 'CUSTOMERS'?

Even if you don't have direct customers, you will have clients and users, who should be treated well, courteously and efficiently. So customer care *is* an issue for you if you are seriously interested in your image and in the good of your organisation.

Every organisation will have a wide range of customers, far more than it at first realises. Everyone with whom you have dealings is a customer of sorts. So remember that as part of the PR mix customer care is not just about the way you treat your obvious 'customers', it is about how you treat anyone you deal with through your work. It is fundamental to your relationships with your many 'publics'. If you have a meeting with someone from another organisation and you are running late, call to say so. Not only is it the polite thing to do, it shows your organisation to be thoughtful and efficient. If you stroll (or indeed rush) in late with no forewarning and no apology, it will give quite a different picture of you and of who you work for.

As well as having many external 'customers' there are also your internal customers – your colleagues. If you work in finance, you probably provide a service to colleagues in other departments. The receptionist, too, is providing a service to others in the organisation. So while you all do different jobs, you work for the same organisation and ultimately you are doing your job to further the aims of the charity. No one should be allowed to see their job in isolation: it needs to be seen as a vital cog in the machine, just as important as all the other cogs, yet useless on its own.

GETTING STARTED

When you are a customer, what things annoy or irritate you? How can you make sure that your organisation is not guilty of these things? Get a friend to ring your charity with a difficult or awkward question and see how they are treated. Get them to write in with a request and see how promptly and efficiently it is handled. Try the same thing with other organisations and see how they compare.

If you go to the supermarket and the cashier ignores you for a few minutes because she is too busy talking to her friend on the next checkout, that gives you a bad impression not only of that cashier, but also of the supermarket as a whole. An organisation is judged by its staff, so the starting point for your own customer care is your reception area and your receptionist/telephonist, because first impressions count.

What image does your reception convey about your organisation? How are your telephones answered? Within three rings? In a friendly way? There's little point in training your receptionist how to be good on the telephone if you don't train staff who pick up extension phones too. The motto 'Dial a smile, don't phone a groan' is a useful one to remember.

Make everything as easy as possible for the people who use your service. A comfortable reception area is important, although it could cost you money to put yours right. There are many things you can do at little or no cost to make life easier and better for your customers. Start by smiling at them – that costs nothing. Next you can make sure that your opening hours are clearly posted, to save people

> ### TRUE STORY
>
> Mr Harold Cottam wrote to the Financial Times as follows: "I am surely not alone in wishing to hang up and phone some other organisation when the person on the other end of the line says: "Hello, thank you for calling the Mucky Sludge Company. This is Kevin/Debbie speaking. How may I help you?"....The person who invented this form of mindless response needs medical treatment urgently." No, Mr. Cottam is not alone. Over-programmed staff are little better than under-trained ones.
>
> So if you are guilty of asking your staff to recite a script when they answer the phone, stop it. Apart from being very boring for the receptionist, it sounds insincere and strips staff of their individuality. It's OK to let people's personality come out when they answer the phone, as long as they respond promptly and in a friendly way.

wasted trips. And how about replying to mail promptly? It costs no more, and it gives a better impression, one of caring efficiency.

SET THE STANDARD

Setting the standard for things like answering the telephone or replying to mail ensures that you have consistent quality throughout the organisation. Specify the standard you expect from staff, and ensure that it is met. When setting standards, always try to quantify it so that it can be measured. For example:

- all telephone calls to be returned within 24 hours
- all mail to be acknowledged within two working days
- telephones to be answered within three rings
- reception to be cleaned at 8.30am each day

You need to set standards, publicise the standards you are aiming for, measure your performance and publish this too. (This may involve nothing more than displaying performance and standards on a noticeboard in your reception.) If you fail to meet your standards, explain why – to users and to staff.

Standards need to be genuine, demanding, yet achievable. Review them if they prove too easy or too ambitious.

Here are some examples of good and bad customer care:

BAD: "She's not here. You'll have to ring back later."

GOOD: "I'm sorry but Janet's out of the office just now. I can take your details and get her to ring you back within the next hour, or perhaps I can help you myself?"

BAD: "It's nothing to do with me. It's not my department."

GOOD: "I'm sorry to hear that our training department made a mistake. I'll have a word with the training manager and ask her to ring you back this afternoon with an explanation of how it happened."

BAD: "You're not the only one who has had to wait three weeks for a copy of our annual report. We do operate on a shoe string, you know, and anyway, I'm only a volunteer."

GOOD: "I'll put a copy in the post to you immediately. Please accept our apologies for the delay."

BAD: "You're got a nerve! You're complaining about a service that you don't even pay for. Most people would show a bit more gratitude."

GOOD: "We take all complaints very seriously. Thank you for telling us about it. We will carry out an investigation and get back to you within a week."

CORPORATE RESPONSIBILITY

The key to handling situations like this is to get your staff to accept corporate responsibility. The customer does not care that you are short-staffed or that you work in another section. They regard you as a representative of the organisation, and therefore they hold YOU responsible. You have to accept that responsibility, with the customer at least. Bawl out one of your colleagues later if you must, but make sure that the customer's problem is sorted out first. Never pass a customer from pillar to post – it will only add to their bad feeling and give them another cause for complaint.

If you want staff to accept corporate responsibility, you need to involve them in the process of improving customer care. Ask them for their ideas on what can be improved (if you're large enough, you could even introduce a staff suggestion scheme), have brainstorming sessions, and tackle problems together.

As well as including staff in coming up with ideas for improved customer care, bring in the real experts – your customers! Ask them what they think, and encourage suggestions (perhaps via a suggestions/comments box) and feedback.

> **TRUE STORY**
>
> An NHS chiropody clinic wanted to provide better customer care. Staff were asked for ideas, and one suggested that the clinic should sell chiropody products to patients at less than the price they could be bought at the chemist. They introduced the idea, which was warmly welcomed by patients. The small profit from the sales was invested in plants and pictures to make the waiting room more comfortable.

CUSTOMER OR CLIENT CHARTERS

Whatever your political persuasion, it's difficult to deny that one of the successes of the Conservative government has been in focusing attention on customers' rights. They launched under the Citizens' Charter a whole series of other charters, such as the Patients' Charter and the Tenants' Charter, which set out clearly what we can expect as consumers of public services. What can your clients expect? Why not commit yourself to a standard and show your customers their rights set out clearly and displayed prominently? It shows your clients that they matter to you.

A Scottish hospital which cares for people with learning disabilities has produced a patients' charter for those with literacy and learning difficulties. Featuring lots of symbols, self-explanatory pictures and images, and clear and simple language, it is a document that is much easier for this particular audience to get to grips with than the standard NHS patients' charter. This example of good practice in customer care illustrates how important it is to tailor materials to the needs of the audience.

CUSTOMER CARE MISSION STATEMENTS

Many companies have mission statements setting out what they are about. Why not produce a customer care mission statement for your charity? My own mission statement for my company is to provide a top quality public relations service that is flexible and responsive to clients' needs and results in complete client satisfaction. What is your customer care mission statement?

BE A COPY CAT

If you come across a customer care idea that works, copy it, adapting it as necessary to fit your organisation. A manager running an NHS chiropody clinic spotted a good idea at her local hairdresser, which showed people before and after their new hair treatment. She adapted this at her clinic to show feet before and after treatment, so that patients would have a clear idea of how their feet would look. This was found to take away much of the fear and anxiety about treatment and to give patients something positive to focus on. Have you encountered any good ideas that would be appropriate in your organisation?

GIVING THEM WHAT THEY NEED

Charities have in the past been accused of being paternalistic, of deciding what is in people's best interests and then giving it to them. Real customer care is not about offering what you believe your clients want, it is about asking them what they need and delivering on that. For many charities this will involve re-focusing and taking your direction from a different source – your customers.

Find out what customers want by asking them. Consider:

- ■ a questionnaire (see chapter 1 for details of how to compile one)
- ■ a seminar for clients/users to say what they want and for you to listen, take note and take action
- ■ a visit to a cross-section of your customers to ask for their views
- ■ a comments and suggestions book
- ■ setting up a customers/users panel

> **TRUE STORY**
>
> **Getting it right:** A woman's father was dying in a hospice. When she went to visit him a friendly nurse brought her a cup of tea and a biscuit. After her father's death the woman donated a substantial part of his estate to the hospice.

> **TRUE STORY**
>
> **Getting it wrong:** A woman called into a local charity shop to drop off a bag of bric-a-brac for sale. The volunteer behind the counter carried on chatting to one of the customers, ignoring the woman, who finally left the shop in disgust, still with her bag. When she got home she cancelled her standing order to the charity and told all of her friends how rude the staff were. Now she never gives to or buys from the shop and she no longer supports the charity. Neither do her friends.

TRUE STORY

A hospital equipped a separate waiting room in casualty specially for children, since it felt that it would be less traumatic for children and their parents to be separated from the adult accident and emergency patients. It decided to fill the room with toys and games to keep the children occupied, but someone suggested that perhaps it would be a good idea to take guidance from parents as to what they would like to see in the room. "A doctor," replied one mother, "for what's the use of toys if my child is too sick to play?" The parents clearly had a different view of need to the hospital authorities. Then they asked the children, who unanimously wanted to see a television and sweets in the waiting room. This was at odds with the view of the parents. The moral? Seek the views of those affected, don't rely on your own guesswork.

HANDLING COMPLAINTS

Organisations new to the concept of customer care think that it's about handling complaints. Real customer care is about organising your group so that you get things right in the first place, thus removing the causes of complaint. Nevertheless, even in the best-run place things will occasionally go wrong, and you need to be geared up to respond properly and to correct errors.

People are generally very reluctant to make formal complaints, although they might well grumble to others about poor service. Of all dissatisfied customers, 96% do not complain, though they do tell seven others how bad you are, and 13% will tell at least 20 others. Companies and commercial organisations are more likely to receive complaints, because their complaints will be coming from people who have paid for something and therefore feel that they have more of a right to expect a certain standard. Charities are extremely unlikely to receive many complaints: they are regarded as doing a worthwhile job, and users of their services feel grateful and think it would be wrong to complain.

If you genuinely care about your customers, encourage them to complain and be sure that you don't regard complaints as threats. Complaints provide you with an opportunity to find out where you are failing and to put it right. Always handle complaints courteously, satisfactorily and promptly. If you run a service, you might wish to draw up an official complaints procedure for your users and to give a copy to everyone. If your clients are vulnerable people, or they lack confidence, you could appoint an independent client advocate to represent them or to help make the complaint. If you run a charity shop, you might find it useful to have a policy covering returned good or refunds. Develop a system that works for your own organisation.

An Edinburgh housing association was concerned that tenants with a learning disability might not make a complaint, either because they were illiterate and could not understand even the plain English complaints leaflet, or because they lacked the confidence to do so. To combat this they produced a complaints video setting out how to make a complaint and showing real life tenants and staff acting out the procedures to explain what happens. This accessible and relevant video is now shown to all new tenants with a learning disability, to ensure that they are familiar with their rights and to make it clear that complaints are genuinely encouraged.

Give your staff guidelines on how to deal with customer complaints, both oral and written. They might be something like this:

GUIDELINES FOR ANSWERING COMPLAINTS OVER THE PHONE

1. However angry or unreasonable you think the caller is, always remain polite and helpful.

2. If there has been a delay in answering the call, or you need to put a caller on hold, apologise for keeping them waiting.

3. If a caller is complaining about something outside the remit of our organisation, explain this to them and point them in the right direction.

4. Never leave a caller feeling that they have been abandoned or dealt with in an unsatisfactory way. Ensure that they get to speak to someone, or that you arrange for someone to call them within a specified time.

> **TRUE STORY**
>
> British Airways carried out a survey among its customers, and discovered that of all those who experience problems but make no complaint, half do not intend to use the airline again. This contrasts with the customers who are dissatisfied and do complain – just 13% of this group will defect, the same rate of defection as among the satisfied group. The lesson? Encourage complaints and use them to help you improve what you do.

5. If it is your fault, always say sorry and offer (without waiting to be asked) to do what you can to put things right.

Many customers will not complain in person at the time, but they will write in afterwards. Dealing with written complaints gives you time to think, so it can be easier than a complaint made face-to-face. However, you need to be careful not to get into a position where letters are toing and froing for months on end because with each letter you are raising more issues than you address.

If the complaint seems to grow with each letter, why not suggest meeting to discuss the problem face-to-face? Always offer to visit the complainant; never expect them to have to come to you, though make that an option. Also make sure that you make yourself available at a time that is most suitable to them, even if it's an evening or weekend. Point out that they can bring someone else to the meeting to support and help represent them. Follow up any meeting with a letter thanking the complainant for their time and summing up the position.

You should ensure that you have a system for copying customer complaints to relevant staff, so that there is an opportunity for a complaint to result in a policy or service delivery change or improvement. If you get a complaint that your opening hours make it very difficult for those working office hours to use your service, you might consider opening late one night a week. This will only come about if the person dealing with the complaint feeds the information through to the relevant committee. I once complained to a hospital that it was inappropriate for them to ask me my marital status; it was a question they would not ask job applicants, so why ask patients? Months later I discovered that they were continuing this practice; no action had been taken as a result of my complaint. The image I had of the hospital was damaged by this discovery, and I was left feeling that they had no genuine interest in patients' views.

Always aim to turn complainants into ambassadors. It can be done, as you can see from the box on the left:

THE DOs AND DON'Ts OF CUSTOMER COMPLAINTS

DO:

- show empathy
- listen
- let them make their case
- sympathise (regardless of where the blame lies)
- apologise – if it was your fault
- propose corrective action
- do more than the minimum
- offer compensation if appropriate

DON'T:

- say "It's not my fault" – remember corporate responsibility
- interrupt – it will infuriate the complainant
- jump to conclusions – they will probably be wrong
- argue – you will gain nothing and will only antagonise
- lose your temper – it won't help
- accept responsibility until you are sure it's your fault – that doesn't stop you from sympathising though

---

TRUE STORY: GETTING IT RIGHT

I ordered some adhesive address labels as a birthday present for a friend, but the company sent the labels to my friend rather than me, thus baffling her (she had no idea where they had come from) and spoiling my gift idea. When I complained by telephone, the company apologised, gave me the labels free, and offered to send me a complimentary set for my own use. They followed this up with a very apologetic letter. I was impressed and will feel confident about using the company again and recommending it to others.

TRUE STORY: GETTING IT WRONG

I had been having problems with my mail for weeks. Some letters took weeks to arrive, some failed to arrive at all, and others were found scattered across the pavement outside the house. I complained to Royal Mail, who said they would investigate. Weeks passed and I heard nothing. I chased them several times and was told that my complaint was still being investigated. More weeks passed. I phoned again only to discover that all the correspondence relating to my complaint had been lost. They eventually admitted that they were in the wrong and had compounded the problem by handling the complaint badly, and having poor systems that led to the papers being lost. They offered me £5 compensation. I pointed out that this derisory sum hardly covered my phone bill to them, let alone the time I had spent pursuing the complaint, or the enormous inconvenience I had been put to. Their response? "We don't have to give you anything at all. This is a goodwill payment." It didn't create any goodwill!

- be patronising – you might get a punch on the nose!
- blame others – remember corporate responsibility again

HAVE A GO YOURSELF

A client has made a complaint about your receptionist and you send the following reply. What is wrong with it?

Dear Mrs. McGinty,

Many thanks for your letter of July 22nd. We note your complaint and apologise for any distress or inconvenience caused.

Please let us know if you have any other suggestions or complaints about our service in the future.

Yours sincerely,

Eileen O'Keefe
Administrative Secretary

There are a number of mistakes with the letter:

- It appears to be a standard letter sent out to all complainants. This makes the complainant feel that:

a) they do not deserve a personal reply

b) you receive lots of complaints and this is the only way you can cope with the volume, by sending standard letters

- The sender of the letter is a junior member of staff, which will make your complainant feel that you do not attach much importance to complaints

- You do not say what you intend to do to remedy the situation/make sure it never happens again

You should be sending letters that are more like this:

Dear Mrs. McGinty,

Thank you for your letter of July 22nd. I was very concerned when I read it and an immediate investigation was carried out.

Our receptionist was asked why she was rude to you. She said she was under considerable stress that day, having received news of the death of a close relative. That is of course no excuse for rudeness, though we hope it goes some way to explaining her out of character behaviour.

As a result of your complaint we will be taking a close look at the training of our reception staff, to ensure that something like this never happens again. Once we have carried out a full review and come up with recommendations for improving our reception service we will contact you again to let you know what action we intend to take. If you have any thoughts or ideas of your own, we would be interested in hearing them.

The receptionist concerned has written a personal letter of apology to you (enclosed).

Please call me if you feel that this complaint has not been dealt with satisfactorily or if you have any other concerns you would like to discuss. My direct line is 967 6784.

Yours sincerely,

Aled Jones
Director

This is better because:

- it clearly demonstrates that complaints are taken seriously and dealt with by senior staff

- it shows that immediate action was taken and follow-up action is planned (it's not enough to take action, you need to tell the complainant what you are doing)

- it gives the complainant an opportunity to discuss it further (an offer which is unlikely to be taken up, though it's still worth making) and to come up with ideas and be involved in making customer care better

Never send out bland and uninformative letters in response to complaints, unless you want to antagonise the complainant. If you need to carry out enquiries before responding fully, always send a holding reply within 48 hours, to show that the complaint isn't being ignored. Say in the holding letter when the complainant can expect to hear from you again.

TRAINING FOR CUSTOMER CARE

At the end of the day it is down to your staff to deliver excellent customer care. They cannot do this by instinct, they need to be shown how. Surveys show that new staff working in shops get only one twelfth as much training in handling people as in handling cash, yet unless they handle people properly they won't be handling much money! Staff who need to use a computer are given computer training, those who interview and appoint staff are given recruitment and selection training, yet staff who deal with the public are not expected to have any special skills – because this activity is regarded as common sense, something we can all do with ease. Yet clearly it's not that easy, for we can all recount horrendous examples of poor customer care. Staff need to be trained in the importance of customer care and in customer care skills.

Each member of staff should be trained, for everyone will come into contact with customers. Many hospitals train nursing staff, receptionists and telephonists in customer care, but they forget about the cleaners, who probably have as much contact with the public as frontline staff. Lost visitors ask them directions all day long, yet without customer care training, cleaners will be unclear about what is expected of them. They will continue to regard visitors' questions as unwelcome interruptions that get in the way of their real task: cleaning the corridors and wards. If customer care is part of everyone's job description (and their appraisal), and everyone learns how to do it, you will begin to see real customer care in action. Remember that once you've got your customer care right, include customer care training as part of the induction process for all new staff. That way you can keep up the standard.

THE FIVE FOUNDATION STONES OF GOOD CUSTOMER CARE

1. Undue staff stress prevents good customer care. Find the causes and, where possible, remove them.

2. Make sure that everyone understands the importance of customer care. Write it into all job descriptions.

3. Involve staff and customers/clients in the development of a customer care programme.

4. Train all staff in customer care – from the bottom to the top.

5. Include customer care training as part of your induction programme, and don't forget training for volunteers.

Ultimately customer care will make things better for your staff as well as your customers, because happy customers are nicer to staff. Angry and frustrated customers will vent their anger on....guess who?

CHAPTER FOURTEEN

USING PR CONSULTANTS

If you are interested in bringing in consultants to help you with your PR, this chapter is a must. It could help prevent you making costly mistakes or getting ripped off, and will show you how to have a successful relationship with a consultancy.

For many voluntary organisations, the idea of employing a PR consultancy is an expensive luxury that they could never afford. If you are not in that group, and you are considering some extra help, what should your first step be?

The first thing to do, before you speak to any consultants, is to be clear about why you need them. What do you hope to achieve? Would it be better to appoint someone in-house, perhaps even as a temporary or part-time post? Once you are certain that you would benefit from using a consultant, write a brief which sets out your objectives, and circulate it to at least three, and preferably six, PR consultants. If you can, approach consultancies recommended to you by people or organisations you trust. If this is not possible, you may have to resort to good old Yellow Pages. Alternatively, ask the Institute of Public Relations (the professional body representing PR consultants – Tel. 0171 253 5151) if they know of anyone in your area who specialises in charity PR. The IPR has a charity group, so they should be able to come up with something helpful.

> **TRUE STORY**
>
> I was looking for a PR agency to award a contract to. I rang a few to ask for their brochure and client list and most were happy to oblige. One, however, quizzed me on why I wanted a brochure, demanded to know who I was, and was generally unhelpful and unfriendly. How could I ask a company to do my PR when they were clearly incapable of doing their own? Although they never knew it, that telephone conversation lost them the chance of £20,000 worth of business.

Most consultancies specialise in business PR and will probably know very little about charities, so try to select a consultancy that already works for a charity or voluntary organisation, or has done so in the past. PR consultancies now realise that the charity sector is a market for them, so finding an agency with relevant experience is easier than it used to be.

What does a PR brief look like? The sample brief on page 188 covers the sorts of things you should include in yours.

Once you have selected your prospective consultants (your shortlist is known as a pitch list) and issued them with the brief, set a deadline and then ask them in to do a presentation to you

> **TIP**
>
> *Consider using a freelance PR consultant, as this can work out much cheaper than an agency. They will have much lower overheads and are more likely to be able to be flexible. The drawback, however, is that they will not have the backing of an organisation and colleagues to fall back on if they are sick or on holiday. Some freelance consultants work with associates, so you can get the best of both worlds with such an arrangement.*

on how they would approach your assignment and what ideas they have. Get them to bring to the presentation a document setting out their approach and detailing their costs. Alternatively, go to their premises for the presentation; it's more time-consuming, but you get a better idea of who you will be doing business with. You do not have to pay a consultancy to do a pitch presentation and they will not expect payment. There is debate within the PR industry about whether consultancies should charge, but this has been going on for years and looks unlikely to be resolved.

You can decide after the presentations whom you want to use, or whittle down your list and receive a further presentation from the best of the bunch. This will give you a chance to digest what you were told last time, and to ask any questions that have since occurred to you. Alternatively, if you are unhappy with all those you have seen, draw up a new pitch list and start again.

When assessing the performance of prospective consultants, ask yourself:

- did they fulfil the requirements of the brief in their tender documents?

- was their presentation confident?

- did they come up with good ideas?

- did they seem personally committed or sympathetic to our cause?

- did they seem to understand what we are about?

- did they handle questions well?

- do I feel, from what I have seen, that I have confidence in them?

In addition to telling your prospective consultants about yourself, you need to know about them. Ask them:

- What experience they have of working for organisations similar to your own. Ask for names of clients and details of projects. Don't hesitate to take up references if you are unsure.

- What knowledge and understanding they have of your subject area. If none of your consultants knows much about your field, ask them how they would go about building up their expertise.

- Who will be working on your account. Ask for their CVs, so you can be sure of their experience. (The people who present to you are not always those who will be carrying out the work.)

- How many staff they have.

- How long they have been established.

- What other clients they work for.

- Are the consultants who would work on your account members of the Institute of Public Relations (IPR)? How long have they been members?

- How they would evaluate the success of the work they carry out for you?

- Has the consultancy won any awards, such as the IPR's Sword of Excellence?

Don't be impressed if a consultancy says that it is a member of the Public Relations Consultancies' Association: this is a trade body set up to represent the interests of its members.

When deciding whom to use, you should obviously pick a competent consultancy, one you have faith in. But cost will be an important factor too. When you are quoted costs for PR consultancy, ask:

- Does this include VAT?

- What do you charge for photocopying, paper, faxes etc.? Are these charged at cost price? (Some consultancies charge exorbitant sums for stationery and administration, so be careful that you are not ripped off in this way.)

- Do you operate a mark-up system when you buy in services such as print or design? If so, what do you mark up by? (Most PR consultancies, if they use a designer, printer or photographer to do work for you, will add anything upwards of 17% to the bill. If your consultancy marks up, organise your own printers etc. if you want to save money and stretch your budget further.)

- What are your hourly rates? (Some consultancies operate an hourly or daily rate, but others charge a retainer. This is a flat monthly rate which you must pay whether or not you make use of your consultant. Retainers are normally charged for on-going support, but a set rate, agreed in advance, will be charged for a project.)

- Do you charge time for travel?

- How do you account for expenditure? Do you issue itemised bills and timesheets?

Most consultancies will ask you what your PR budget is, and you will certainly need to have decided this internally. Whether you choose to share this information with a prospective consultant is up to you.

WORKING WITH CONSULTANTS

Once you have selected a consultancy, you need to make sure that you get the best out of it. For the relationship to work, your consultancy will need to have clear guidelines from you on what they can and can't do, and you will need to agree a work plan with them, with timescales and budgets.

Regular meetings with your consultants are a must. You need to keep them informed and they will need to brief you on the work they have carried out to date. Most will provide you with a "contact report" after each meeting. Rather like minutes, this will set out in note form what was agreed and who is to do it.

If you enter into a long-term contract with a consultant, make sure that you meet after three or six months specifically to review the work and

---

THE DOG'S DINNER:
BRIEF FOR PUBLIC RELATIONS SUPPORT

ABOUT US

The Dog's Dinner is a dogs' home for abandoned dogs. A registered charity, we currently house around 100 dogs in our kennels in Twickenwich. We receive 10% of our funds in the form of grants from the local authority; we get the remainder from charitable donations.

We never turn dogs away and we never have them put down. Our aim is to find homes for all our dogs, but if this is not possible, we keep them for their lifetime.

OUR PR OBJECTIVES

We are seeking to appoint a PR consultant, initially for six months, who can work with us to:

1. Raise our profile in the city, so we can attract more donations. We aim to increase donations by 10% this year.

2. Raise awareness of what we do, so that more people will approach us offering to give a dog a home. We aim to increase the number of dogs we find homes for each year from 75 to 95.

3. Get the amount of funding we receive from the council increased by 10%. Our target is to reach councillors on the grants committee and to show them what a good job we are doing and how our funding needs to be increased if we are to continue our work.

Following an assessment and evaluation after six months, we may decide, funding permitting, to extend the contract.

OUR BUDGET

In addition to the costs of employing a consultant, we have around £500 to spend on PR during the first six months.

check that you are happy with them and that everything is on target. Many consultants organise such review meetings as a matter of course, and may even ask you to complete a customer satisfaction questionnaire at this stage. If yours does not, why not suggest that they do?

Never sign a contract with a consultancy that will commit you to them for more than a year, and always ensure that anything you do sign has a get-out clause, enabling you to terminate the contract, with due notice. Remember that PR is a buyer's market and there will always be consultants out there eager to help you, so do not remain with an agency if you are unhappy with them. Discuss the problems, and if they cannot be resolved, go elsewhere.

Having found a consultancy you are happy with, it generally makes sense to stick with them. The longer you use them, the more they will come to know and understand your work. There is, though, always the danger that they will become complacent, and for this reason, you might decide to ask them to take part in a competitive re-pitch for your account every three years. Many companies and public bodies employ this practice with their consultants to keep them on their toes and to ensure that they are getting the best deal.

Although your consultant is a supplier and not an employee, remember that they need to know what you are up to, just as a member of staff would. Tell them when your office is shutting down for a holiday, tell them if a new trustee or key member of staff is to be appointed, tell them if you are planning something major, get them on your regular mailing list. If you want to ensure that you get the best out of your consultants, keep them informed. They can't come up with ideas for you if you don't tell them your plans. Make sure, too, that they keep you in the picture, particularly where your budget is concerned. If you have a set PR budget, ask your consultants to let you know when half of it is spent, and to give you a countdown as it runs out. If they don't, you may suddenly find that the budget is gone and you're only half way through the year.

> **TIP**
>
> *Some PR consultancies will consider doing their bit for the community by giving free PR support to local charities. You might want to see if any consultancies in your area are so public-spirited, though bear in mind that they will probably support you only if you have 'appeal' (this generally refers to animals or children) and are not in any way controversial. You'll also need to be the sort of charity that will enhance their image in some way, or that will result in some good press for them.*

> **TRUE STORY**
>
> A retail company looking for PR support was invited to the offices of one of the PR consultancies pitching for this lucrative account. The receptionist ignored the company directors for several minutes while she finished a phone call to a friend. The directors were then kept waiting for a further 30 minutes by the PR consultants. Finally, when they were on the verge of leaving in disgust, the consultants asked them through to the meeting room. "We decided to treat you the way you treat your customers, just so you know how they feel," said one of the PR people. "Use us and we'll help you tackle your poor customer care and your bad image." They won the account! Good PR professionals will help you see things through clients' eyes.

USEFUL ADDRESSES AND PUBLICATIONS

This is not a comprehensive list, though it covers some of the main companies and organisations you may need to contact, as well as the key publications:

THE PUBLIC RELATIONS INDUSTRY

The Institute of Public Relations
The Old Trading House
15 Northburgh Street
London EC1V 0PR
Tel. 0171 235 5151
Web site http://www.ipr.press.net

This is the professional body which represents around 5,000 PR professionals.

The Public Relations Consultants' Association
Willow House
Willow Place
Victoria
London SW1P 1JH
Tel. 0171 233 6026

The PRCA can help you find a PR consultancy, for they run a free referral service, though they will only recommend their members, who tend to be the more expensive consultancies.

IPR Journal
This quarterly publication is published by the IPR.

PR Week
174 Hammersmith Road
London W6 7JP
Tel. 0171 413 4520

The weekly magazine for people working in PR. Covers charity as well as commercial PR issues.

PRESS CUTTINGS BUREAUX

Romeike and Curtice
Hale House
290-296 Green Lanes
London N13 5TP
Tel. 0181 882 0155
Web site http://www.romeike.com

Durrant's Press Cuttings Limited
103 Whitecross Street
London EC1Y 8QT
Tel. 0171 588 3671

The Broadcast Monitoring Company
89½ Worship Street
London EC2A 2BE
Tel. 0171 377 1742

EDS Presscuttings
25-27 Easton Street
London WC1X 0DS
Tel. 0171 278 8441

McCallum Media Monitor
10 Possil Road
Glasgow G4 9SY
Tel. 0141 333 1822

Paperclip Partnership
Unit 9
The Ashway Centre
Elm Crescent
Kingston-upon-Thames
Surrey KT2 6HH
Tel. 0181 549 4857

All of the above offer a national service and some have local offices.

Clipability
39–41 Carrholm Road
Leeds LS7 2NQ
Tel. 0113 269 3290
(North of England papers only)

BROADCAST MONITORING

The Broadcast Monitoring Company
89½ Worship Street
London EC2A 2BE
Tel. 0171 247 1166

Tellex Monitors
Communications House
210 Old Street
London EC1V 9UN
Tel. 0171 556 3100

The above offer a national service, and also have offices in the North of England and Scotland.

VIDEO NEWS RELEASES

Medialink
14 Soho Square
London W1V 5FB
Tel. 0171 439 1774

TV News London Limited
4 Millbank
London SW1P 3JA
Tel. 0171 222 0807

Reuters Television
40 Cumberland Avenue
London NW10 7EH
Tel. 0171 510 7534

COMPLAINTS ABOUT THE MEDIA

The Press Complaints Commission
1 Salisbury Square
London EC4Y 8AE
Tel. 0171 353 1248

The Broadcasting Complaints Commission
35 and 37 Grosvenor Gardens
London SW1W 0BS
Tel. 0171 630 1966